MORE THAN SKIN DEEP

MARGARET ARMITAGE

AN OMF BOOK

First published 1988

OMF Books are distributed by
OMF, 404 South Church Street,
  Robesonia, Pa. 19551, USA;
OMF, Belmont, The Vine,
  Sevenoaks, Kent, TN13 3TZ, UK;
OMF, P.O. BOX 177, Kew East,
  Victoria 3102, Australia;
and other OMF offices.

ISBN 9971-972-67-0

Printed in Singapore   SNP 10K 4/88

CONTENTS

Foreword

This story is perhaps best described as "fictionalized fact". It is true in the sense that all the main events really happened in the lives of some of my closest friends in Central Thailand. For the overall narrative I do have three real people in mind, but I have woven the experiences of others into their lives, with the aim of making the story both more informative and more entertaining. Most of the names are fictitious; I have retained the real names of a few who are only mentioned briefly and about whom the information is a hundred percent accurate.

Most of the dialogue and implied gestures are necessarily fabricated, and some of the incidents described are embellished out of my own imagination. I feel that this is unavoidable if the story is to come alive. However, if I can say this without being presumptuous, I dare to conclude that the supposed thoughts, reactions, behaviour and everyday situations that these people faced before I knew them could really have taken place as set out here. This is Thai life.

This book is not being written merely as a tear jerker to gain sympathy for a group of the world's disadvantaged persons. Rather it aims to illustrate what can be done for them in these days of modern medicine and advancement in reconstructive surgery. It seeks to emphasize how men and women have been reclaimed from the ravages of the malicious disease of leprosy, and draws attention to efforts being made to integrate them into normal society.

The Thai government, encouraged by the World Health Organization, has passed various laws to try to ensure that one-time leprosy sufferers, now free from infection of leprosy though still having left-over deformities, will once again become integrated members of society. The Health Department spends a considerable amount of money to educate the general public about this disease through the medium of radio and TV. The king and queen of Thailand have a special concern for leprosy sufferers, and make an effort to visit leprosy hospitals and villages from time to time. Such visits are always shown on television.

Consequently, ex-leprosy sufferers are now much more acceptable to normal society than they were a few years ago. However, the vast majority of mankind worldwide has a built-in repulsion mechanism that works overtime when face to face with the abnormal, the disfigured or the unlovely. A policy of integration, therefore, does not easily become practice.

What greater challenge then for the church of Jesus Christ here in Thailand to be leaders in receiving non-infectious leprosy people. We do not use the term leper these days.

It is hard to advise about the correct pronounciation of Thai words. In name words the emphasis usually falls on the second syllable, eg Sa*mart*, La*mon*, Ta*wat*. By practising this stress pattern readers may be helped to differentiate automatically between long and short vowels. Many place names of Thai cities have the suffix "BURI", eg LOPBURI, SARABURI, SINGBURI, INBURI. This syllable "Buri" (again with stress on second syllable) means FORTRESS. Interestingly, in some of these towns, there are obvious remains of ancient city walls, easily three feet thick and very high with tall battlements still erect after a thousand years. Lopburi is a particularly good example of a well-fortified city.

Thai spelling often uses th, ph, etc to show aspirated consonants, but this "h" is not pronounced.

Because of unavoidable delays on a number of occasions, it has taken several years to bring this book into being. Therefore my greatest thanksgiving is to God Himself for giving both assurance that this story is worth telling, and also perseverence to a person with my temperament.

Many thanks to Alan Bennett (OMF Superintendent in Central Thailand a few years ago) who took me seriously when I joked to him that I was going to write a book. He encouraged me to take myself seriously and have a go, and initiated my getting started. My great appreciation to Edyth Banks (OMF International Editor) who showed enthusiasm when she read the initial outline of my story, and has continued to encourage me over the years. Edyth has always shown she had faith in me, and never seemed to doubt that a book would one day materialize.

Mr Lance Pierson gave me much practical help as a consultant while I was in England in 1985. I'm grateful for his ability to help me to edit my own work. Lance's interest in the story led him to ask questions about the characters and about Thailand which triggered my imagination all over again, so that an improved manuscript came into being.

My friends here in Central Thailand have supported me one hundred percent. So, my grateful thanks to all these and a number of friends around the world who have prayed for me and for this book. Your patience has been admirable.

PART I

Chapter 1
Introducing Samart

The home-made canoe meandered across the sea of placid water, heading for a tiny hamlet snuggled in a semi-circular range of hills in a remote corner of Thailand.

Even though the younger boy in the canoe was only five years old, he handled his oar skilfully as he sat cross-legged up front. Goy loved the water; he knew the first thing he would do when they reached home would be to jump in and swim around to his heart's content. He smiled happily at the thought of seeing his friends and playing with them in the cool water. These youngsters were still completely carefree, indifferent to the hard circumstances that made their parents struggle year after year to make ends meet.

As the little craft made its way slowly towards the village, Goy could peer down into the water and, murky as it was, see the lively fish darting about just below the surface. Sometimes he would plunge his hand into the water in hopes of just "happening" to catch a fish!

Today the sky was overcast, the tropical sun hidden by a thin curtain of cloud. The heat and humidity were oppressive and exhausting. "I wish it would rain," murmured Samart, as his expertise with one oar kept the craft moving steadily forward.

Samart was ten years old, the eldest in his family. He was a thoughtful boy, very capable, and willing to help whenever he could. He was already becoming aware that life wasn't all play. His father needed him to do many jobs and he had to work hard even when he wasn't at school.

"Little brother, do some rowing and help us to get home quickly," he said impatiently to Goy. Not that he was in a hurry to reach home - the situation there wasn't very attractive - but he was hot and sticky and tired. He too badly needed a swim in the refreshing water.

Today, as Samart sat astern in his little canoe and gently paddled her towards the mountain, he was even more thoughtful than usual. Yesterday a new baby had arrived. This meant four children in their family - himself the eldest, Ploy his sister aged seven, young Goy and the new baby.

She's a nice little thing, he told himself, *dainty and pretty, and soon I shall be able to cuddle her. But she won't be a baby for long. Soon she will grow up and need proper food.*

Proper food was often a talking point in his family. It was not easily come by! In those days of 1943 Samart didn't know anything about politics. He didn't really understand when he heard people talk about "the war". What he did know from grass roots experience was that life was hard. His father had to use initiative and put his hand to a variety of jobs to feed his hungry family. Sometimes he made rice noodles to sell for a tiny profit in the nearest small market town. Sometimes Samart had to go with his dad up the forested hills around them to collect wood, which they made into charcoal and sold.

Added to these practical difficulties, another uneasy feeling niggled inside him some days. His mother often wasn't well. He didn't know what was wrong with her, but sometimes he felt very anxious as he saw her breathless and in pain, always pale and weak. No wonder that, as he thought of the baby, further apprehension was born in his heart. He had enough foresight to realize that a new sister would soon require rice and all the other things to go with it. His mother had told him that after the baby was born, she would feel stronger and able to work again. *I do hope so,* he sighed.

This leisurely journey took place far out in the western part of Lopburi province, at the southern end of one of the vast rice bowls of Asia - the plains of central Thailand. It was before the days of man-made irrigation systems. So some years, as this one, there was excessive flooding and the rice was drowned. Other years the earth dried up after initial rain and rice planting; then with insufficient rainfall during the following months, the rice was scorched to death. The right amount of rain could not be guaranteed in this isolated spot, fifteen degrees north of the equator.

"Goy, make sure you salute the Buddha as we come in line with the hillside idol," Samart called to his young brother, breaking the silence between them.

This Buddha image high above their home was only one of a number of Buddhist effigies and pagodas strewn across the landscape. They were accessories to three majestic Buddhist temples erected on rocky prominences across the hillsides. At the appropriate moment both boys laid aside their oars and without any embarrassment, bowed their heads and raised their hands in a *wai,* the Thai sign of reverence - palms together, finger-tips adjacent to chin.

As the boat neared their home, Goy stood up, "Here we are at last," he shouted, his face screwed up with delight as he anticipated the joy of playing in the water.

He quickly peeled off his sleeveless vest and short scanty pants, leaving Samart to manoeuvre the canoe into the sandy lower slopes of the hillside. There he stood, his light brown body quite naked, poised with hands raised above his head, ready to jump into the inviting water. "Come and swim, big brother," he shouted as Samart tied up the boat.

"I'm going to see how mother is and look at the baby first," Samart called as he went up the steps into the house, which was built on stilts high above the ground.

After chatting with his mother he took a peep at his baby sister. At ten years old he felt he had some kind of special relationship with her. She was different from Ploy and Goy. When they were born he had still been small himself. But he felt responsible to take care of this new sister.

In the following months, Samart's mother did become stronger. The baby thrived and quickly became the centre of attraction. As her personality blossomed, it became apparent that her name, Lamon, was appropriate: it meant pleasant, gentle, beautiful, polite. They were a happy family, and in spite of continuing hardships, the children were secure in the love and dependability of their parents.

Samart enjoyed school; he was bright and well able to cope with his lessons. So it was a great blow when, a year after Lamon's birth, he had to leave school. He was eleven and had completed his four years of compulsory education. There was no high school nearby, and anyway he was needed at home to contribute to the family budget.

"Your father didn't sleep last night," Mother said anxiously one morning, three years later. "Now he has a bad headache and a fever."

Samart went over to where his father was lying on his straw mat. "Shall I go to the doctor and bring some medicine for you?" he asked. The older man's expression showed the severe pain he was feeling, and as Samart bent lower he could see even in the dim early morning light how pale his father looked.

"Wait a while, son," he said weakly, "I shall be better in a few hours. Go get wood, and make a fire for your mother. Tell Ploy to get the rice ready for cooking."

"Lamon, come with me," Samart took her hand as he went towards the steps. She needed no second invitation; she worshipped her big brother and went everywhere possible with him. As he bent to chop a log into slivers for kindling, she squatted beside him, keeping up animated conversation all the while. He never lost patience with her endless questions. She was a delightful little girl and he loved her very much.

Breakfast consisted of a tasty omelette and fish soup with bamboo shoots, to go with their large helpings of rice. There was plenty for everyone.

"Goy," whispered Samart as his young brother was leaving for school, "please call and tell our uncle that father isn't well; he may come and persuade him to send for medicine."

As the hours rolled by, Father did not improve. Uncle came to visit about midday, by which time the family were very anxious. Father had a raging fever, and the pain in his head was worse than ever. He didn't have to be persuaded to allow Samart to go for the doctor, who was really no more than a medicine man, a specialist in herbs. Sometimes his treatment worked well, but all too often it was inadequate to treat severe tropical infections, and it was always expensive. He came at once to visit the patient.

"Samart, take these leaves and boil them in the largest pan you can find," ordered the doctor. "The pan must be filled to the brim with water." Samart had often watched his father prepare such potions, when the doctor had prescribed them for Mother. Now he had to do it himself. The brew began to release an unpleasant odour as steam rose. It simmered for half an hour.

"We have to wait a while for it to cool," explained the medicine man. "But as soon as the sediment has settled to the bottom, you can take out a cupful of the clear liquid. It has to be mixed with liquor and then it will be ready to drink."

The medicine was ineffective, and Father died two days later.

Mother managed to maintain a calm facade, but inside her heart was breaking. Her husband had been loving and kind, and had always done what he could to keep the heavy work from her. No matter how often things went wrong he always had new ideas; he always knew what to do to earn money for food. Now he was gone.

The three older children also knew clearly what this sudden loss of their father would mean. Even four-year-old Lamon understood the word "death" to mean that Dad would not be coming home ever again.

Samart's uncle and aunt and other more distant relatives were all sympathetic and helpful in organizing the funeral. The various Buddhist merit-making ceremonies would continue for a whole week.

One of the nearby temples was particularly beautiful and ornate, its extensive grounds very peaceful. Samart often went there; he knew some of the monks, and enjoyed chatting with them. He learned a lot about his national religion from the head monk of that temple; they were good friends. It was here that his father would be cremated on the seventh day after his death.

However, during those days of merit-making for his father, this was not the temple that suited Samart's mood. He was feeling very lonely. Relatives and friends calling in meant that the house always seemed full of people; yet no one had time for him. So most days he made his escape and took Lamon with him, as her contented spirit and never-ending banter had a calming effect on him. They would climb the hill to the other temple which had an air of grandeur. It was built high up on a great prominence of rock. The main building, tall and stately, could be seen for miles around. Inside the rock supporting this temple was an extensive cave, divided into rooms by columns of stone and boulders that had been there for centuries. Some of the rooms were rather dark and scary, but Samart wasn't frightened. It was cool and quiet, exactly the kind of place he needed to sit and think. And Lamon loved this cave; she could play to her heart's content.

Sometimes Samart sat in its entrance and gazed out across the field. Sometimes he relaxed and lay down on the cool floor, staring up at the boulders and intricacies of the rock formation high above. To begin with, he felt depressed and anxious, wondering how ever the family would cope without a father. But as he returned to his hideaway time and again, the uneasy feeling began to give way to positive thinking. He built castles in the air - seeing himself doing all the things his father had taught him since he left school. He imagined himself taking initiative and making decisions.

So, when the seventh day arrived, he was ready to

take his place with his mother and uncle and other mourners in the funeral procession, and finally watch the horrific spectacle of his father's body being burned. From that day Samart became a man. He began to practise all he had imagined in his daydreams. Mother's health was not the best, but she worked hard when she was fit, giving Samart help and support, and advice when he needed it. But Samart, aged fourteen, was the breadwinner and head of the family.

Chapter 2
What is wrong with Lamon?

"**M**other, what is this pale mark on Lamon's skin?" Samart asked one day, about a year after Father's death.

"I don't know, son," was Mother's reply, as she tried to sound indifferent. She had already become aware of the patch, and realized it could be the forerunner of a dreadful disease. So dreadful that she didn't dare think of the consequences.

"If the mark persists, we will take Lamon to the medicine man, but not yet," she told Samart. "Don't worry, son; lots of people have dry and discoloured skin in our climate. It may get better on its own, when the weather changes."

The mark on Lamon's arm did not disappear, however. Samart continued to watch it, and so did Mother. In fact it was slowly spreading out and becoming bigger. Samart sensed that his mother did not wish to discuss Lamon's condition, so he kept quiet.

"Does your arm itch, Lamon?" he asked his sister one day. He imagined any patch of dry skin must be irritable.

"No, my skin doesn't itch at all." Samart shrugged. *She should know,* he thought. *She's six years old.* So he didn't argue.

One fateful day he discerned three tiny new pale patches. The initial macule was now almost an inch in diameter and very noticeable. The new, pea-size marks were festooned around the original like satellites. Very faint, but undoubtedly real.

Mother knew that Samart was worried about his sister's skin condition. He wanted her to grow up attractive, with a beautiful complexion. He imagined that his mother did not take Lamon to the doctor because they were increasingly short of money, so he never dared to persuade her. However, agony and turmoil were growing in her heart as she too observed the new lesions.

One day, when Samart was away for several hours, Mother took Lamon to the temple where the head monk was their good family friend. She wanted his opinion of Lamon's condition. This man had no expert medical knowledge, but he knew as well as she did that the marks on Lamon's arm were very suspicious, and could be the early stages of one of the most dreaded diseases in the world. He didn't wish to send Lamon to the medicine man, fearing that if he agreed with the diagnosis, he would reject the family.

The abbot did know of a little technique that had worked successfully for some people, with no further trouble. So he offered this service for Lamon if Mother wished him to try.

"I can't do it immediately; it will take a day or two to prepare the treatment," he told her. "Come back in three days and I will be ready."

The abbot gathered some medicinal leaves and grasses, which he dried in the sun till they became brittle and could be easily crushed to powder. Finally he mixed them to a paste with a natural searing medicine that is not dangerous, but burns when applied to the skin for a lengthy period.

"Samart, I took your little sister to see the Reverend Father at the temple today," Mother called immediately she heard her son arriving home. She was so relieved to find the monk willing to help Lamon that her story came out thick and fast.

Samart was delighted too, though he didn't understand what would happen as a result of the treatment; Mother purposely neglected to explain. Of course Samart insisted that he go along to the temple too on the appointed day.

The abbot was waiting for them, the paste prepared and made into a poultice ready to be bandaged at the site of the macules. He gave them strict instructions that Lamon must not play in water or get the bandage wet when taking a bath; in addition, she must keep it clean.

"The poultice must stay on for seven days," he told them. "Whatever it feels like, it must not come off."

Day one, day two - no adverse reaction from Lamon. Day three - minor complaints of a burning sensation, but not very troublesome. Day four - considerable grumbling! Lamon's arm now very irritable, strong pleas to remove the poultice. Day five and six proved to be a battle of wits, as the family struggled to persuade Lamon to keep the bandage on. At last they took the screaming child to the temple in the hope that the abbot would stop the treatment.

"I cannot remove the poultice today," he told them. "It must stay on for one more day. But here is some medicine for Lamon to drink; it should sooth and relieve the soreness and make her drowsy."

Fortunately, he knew how to cope with the unhappy little girl. He chatted and consoled her until she became quite calm and cooperative, and promised she would not try to take the bandage off.

"Tomorrow is the seventh day; come back in the evening. Then we will get rid of this poultice and I will have some cool, soothing ointment ready."

Mother knew what the result of this treatment would be. Samart realized that something drastic was happening inside the bandage, but he was not prepared for what he saw when the poultice was removed. Gone were the innocent-looking pale patches, and in their place a deep, sloughing ulcer at least one and a half inches across.

"Here is the ointment," said the abbot quickly, "and we have to put another bandage on." As though sensing Samart's shock he continued, "If you bring Lamon here on alternate days, I will change the dressing. It should be healed in two more weeks if we keep it clean."

Samart was relieved to hear that, though he wondered whether it would really heal in only two weeks! To Lamon it sounded almost like a death sentence. She feared that the soreness and burning would get even worse. And still no swimming or playing in the water!

The abbot's prophecy proved remarkably accurate. The ulcer did heal within two weeks. It dried up without complications; no further treatment required.

"How long will it take for this scar tissue to disappear?" Samart asked the abbot.

"It may take a while," he replied vaguely, not wishing to commit himself. "Don't worry, it will gradually fade away." Samart was not so sure, but as there was nothing else to be done he took Lamon home.

"This ugly scar," he said to his mother. "It's like a giant vaccination mark." He sighed and added with frustration, "Vaccination scars never go away. Perhaps it would have been better to leave the faint white patches. They weren't very obvious, but this may never disappear."

His mother tried to console him. "The scar is high on her arm; it won't be seen when she wears her blouse for school."

As for Lamon, she couldn't care less about the scar. She didn't ask whether it would disappear or not. She had more important matters on her mind: she could swim again!

But from this time on, Mother's health began to deteriorate. She became weak and intensely depressed. She seemed to lose the will to live, and died during the following cool season, when Lamon was seven years old.

The children had become a family of orphans.

"Have you heard? The mother of Samart has died!"

"Yes, I've heard. I suppose we must help those children with the funeral arrangements. I feel very sorry for them."

"Samart will want a full-length funeral. He's very proud; he will want his mother to have the best."

"That's true, but they are still in debt from the time their father died. I've heard their uncle in the next village may not be able to pay out for another seven-day funeral for them."

So said the neighbours when news of Mother's death sped around the village. Because the family owned a few acres of land for security, Samart was able to borrow more money; and his mother had an honourable funeral, with suitable merit-making ceremonies carried out by the Buddhist monks.

Yes, they were now a family of orphans! Extremely

poor. The house they lived in was their own, but badly in need of repair. They also owned enough land to plant rice; and if the rainfall was right, they could harvest just about enough to satisfy their needs and keep the hunger pangs away. But the rainfall was often not right, so they were not highly motivated to transplant the seedlings in well-spaced, tidy rows which would give maximum yield for their efforts. They simply sowed the seeds and left the rice to grow until harvest.

Samart was now seventeen. Ploy at fourteen was already very adept at looking after the house, cooking and doing jobs around the farm to help Samart, as well as caring for Lamon. Goy was twelve and had finished school, while Lamon at seven was just ready to start.

With Mother gone, Samart now became even more authoritative. He was very strict and easily showed his displeasure when Ploy and Goy didn't do their jobs properly. His proud and independent streak seemed to grow stronger by the day. He was determined that he and his family would fend for themselves; he was sure they could survive. Even though he was sometimes bossy and aggressive with Ploy and Goy, they never held it against him; they knew as well as he did that their survival depended on themselves. So, in spite of their normal teenage desires and diversions, they cooperated with him. After all, he wasn't always hard and domineering; much of the time he was loving and tenderhearted.

Chapter 3
A sinister development

"**M**art," called Ploy to her brother one morning as she helped her young sister get dressed for school, "come look at Lamon." What Samart saw made his stomach turn over.

"How long have these been here?" he demanded as he looked at the skin abnormalities on his little sister's buttocks.

"I don't know; I've only just seen them," Ploy told him. "I help Lamon to have a bath and get ready every morning, but I haven't noticed these marks before."

There were three new lesions, quite different from the earlier marks on her arm. These patches were pink and slightly raised; the well-defined edges were like a puffy red ring.

"And look," he exclaimed, as his eyes quickly went from her buttocks to take a fresh look at her arm, "here's a similar pink mark round the edge of the burn scar!" *There must be some connection*, he told himself. *Whatever this disease is, it's spreading all over her body.* "Go to school, little sister," he said to Lamon. "Then this afternoon we will go to the temple; the Reverend Father will advise us what to do."

Samart and Ploy both carried heavy hearts that day. They said very little to each other and even young Goy sensed anxiety in the atmosphere. Burning out the original macules had evidently not brought the disease under control after all; it was spreading to other parts of her body. *Was it anxiety about Lamon that caused Mother's untimely death?* he wondered. And the abbot often enquired after Lamon, so Samart knew that he too was still concerned about her. Thoughts like these spiralled in his mind all day as Samart tried to concentrate on his work.

"Why doesn't someone explain more about this disease?" he questioned aloud to no one in particular. "The sudden appearance of these new symptoms makes it seem so sinister!"

Lamon was alert and cheerful, a favourite with people all round the village. She showed promise of doing well at school just as her brothers and sister had done. So that morning she went happily to school. At eight years old she was not worried about herself in the least; she felt fine and couldn't understand why big brother was so anxious. And the prospect of visiting their friend the Reverend Father after school was a delightful one. It would be like a family outing, as all four of them ofen visited the temple together. The abbot had become like a real father to them; they all loved him as much as he obviously loved and cared for them. The temple grounds were so pleasant and peaceful, and the other monks and nuns also showed affection to this family of orphans. Lamon felt nothing but pleasure and excitement all day.

"I will go with you to visit the medicine man," was the abbot's quick decision when he saw the new lesions. "We must discuss what to do and how to treat Lamon."

So off they all went immediately, walking further round the mountain to find the doctor. The two men took considerable time to discuss Lamon's symptoms; they didn't invite the family to join their conversation. Samart, sitting with his back to them, could hear snippets of their discussion - enough to know that they agreed about the diagnosis, and that the doctor was reacting with alarm as he sent Lamon away to play and didn't seem to want to touch her. A new word kept wafting into his range of hearing - the men spoke about *Rook Khi Thut*, which he understood to be the name of the disease, but it meant nothing to him. No doubt the abbot would soon explain.

"What are we going to do about money?" ventured Ploy as the medicine man began to prepare a variety of his dried herbs. She knew from previous experience that he would be asking some exorbitant price.

"We haven't got any money, so if he won't wait for payment, we can't take the medicine." Samart hated to go into further debt, but he desperately wanted to see Lamon healed.

The abbot received the medicines and was preparing to leave.

"That will be 250 baht," said the doctor baldly.

"Two hundred and fifty!" echoed Samart and Ploy together. "We haven't got any money at the moment."

"You will have to borrow it, then," he said, his features hardening by the second.

"We are already in debt to our uncle; we haven't finished paying for the funerals of our parents," Ploy blurted out, tears threatening.

"You can pay me with a sack of rice, then," responded the doctor, still without sympathy.

"A whole sack of rice!" wailed Goy. "We haven't much left for ourselves, and it's months till harvest."

"Your family must have a lot of ill fate from a previous existence," retorted the doctor cynically. "You are going to have to pay out much more money to make merit before your sister will get better from this disease."

"Well, what is this disease, then?" Samart demanded tensely, his temper rising. "Why doesn't someone explain to us what it is?"

"You'll know before long, I think," the medicine man laughed, the hard, callous look again in his face. "You can take the medicine at once," he told them, "but bring the rice tomorrow."

Ploy was crying now; Samart was perplexed, his face flushed with anger, but he had no answer for this unfeeling older man who had the upper hand and seemed to have taken a dislike to them. Goy was bewildered about having to pay such a massive sum for Lamon's medicine. Why such a fuss? After all, she only had a few marks on her skin! He suddenly blurted out,

"Big brother, why do we bother to take this man's medicine? He couldn't cure father or mother; that's why we are so poor and in debt. This medicine for Lamon is probably no better."

After an embarrassed silence, Samart severely reprimanded his brother. But as the truth of what Goy had said began to sink in, the doctor turned on him with a shower of abuse.

The abbot put his arm around Samart's shoulder and called Goy to stand beside him. He knew the other man was wild with anger, and felt these two boys needed his protection. As he hoped, his saffron-robed figure relieved the tension.

If the doctor had been tempted to any violent action, he managed to restrain himself and recover his composure. He laughed again, more humorously now, as though he realized the foolishness of taking offence at a child's remark.

"Goy, you are only thirteen," he said, "but you are clever and shrewd. You are going to be like your big brother." Goy's outburst had suddenly become a great joke to him; he was laughing heartily now. Everyone relaxed, though they hardly dared to laugh with him. His laughter and joking became his own face-saving mechanism.

Then an amazing thing happened. "All right," he said, "you don't need to pay me with rice; you can pay me 150 baht as soon as possible." He hesitated as he watched their frowns and apprehension turn to smiles. "But," he continued, his voice stern again, "I don't want that little girl on my property any more. If my medicine is any good for her, Goy can come for another supply. I absolutely forbid Lamon to come here again."

Samart was extremely puzzled. *Everyone enjoys Lamon, she's a pleasant little girl. Why, why, why is he so much against her?* However, he wasn't about to start another conversation with this man; he wanted to leave as soon as possible. So they all thanked him and left.

It was almost dark as they walked away. Samart was anxious to talk to his abbot friend about the seriousness of Lamon's condition, so they arranged to meet at the temple next morning.

Making the herbal medicine was no problem, but they hadn't reckoned with trying to persuade a little girl who felt perfectly well, to drink the nasty brew. She couldn't even see for herself the large, angry lesions on her buttocks. The others did manage to persuade her to take a little of it that first evening, but Samart knew it would need much patience to coax her into drinking all of it during the next few days. He was quite determined that she would drink it all - he wasn't about to throw away 150 baht.

Next morning Samart was off early to visit the abbot. Although the monk was now more convinced than ever about Lamon's developing disease, he still couldn't bring himself to be totally honest with Samart.

Although he had no medical training, the physical symptoms told him what the disease was. But he was a Buddhist monk in a saffron robe, and his Buddhist religion told him that this disease came as punishment for great wickedness in a previous existence. It was hard to believe that Lamon or anyone from this hard-working, upright family had been reincarnated from anything so evil as that. Perhaps he and the medicine man might be proved wrong, and the symptoms would go away without further disruption to Lamon's life.

To all Samart's questions, therefore - about what symptoms might follow, about the name of the disease, *Rook Khi Thut*, about the doctor's radically changed attitude towards Lamon - the monk managed to give vague answers. He encouraged Samart to believe in the medicine they had received.

"Some people, of course, would organize a special merit-making ceremony," the abbot murmured in a hesitant tone. "But as your finances are so difficult this year, I think you should wait for a while."

"I will discuss it with my uncle," said Samart without enthusiasm.

"No, no!" came the abbot's shocked response. "Don't mention it to anyone yet. Better not to speak about Lamon's symptoms unless anyone sees or asks about them."

Samart walked home in a despondent mood. No

satisfactory answers to his questions; just more worries. Should he try to raise yet more money for a special merit-making ceremony, and so gain favour with the unseen powers that rule the world? The abbot had advised against it for the time being, but Samart felt he must consider the possibility if Lamon did not recover soon.

Why did he suggest a merit-making ceremony, he wondered as he trudged along the dusty path, *and then in the next breath warn against speaking to anyone about my sister's symptoms?* Normally he could trust his abbot friend and depend on him for everything. But today he could not understand the monk's attitude. Samart felt confused and depressed and very sorry for himself.

After reaching home he began on his daily chores, and as he worked, his mind was going at a tangent. *150 baht to find for the medicine man. Better than 250, I suppose; but where shall we get it from? If I'm not to tell uncle about Lamon's symptoms, then I can't borrow from him.* In fact he didn't want to borrow any more from his uncle; the debt for the funerals was already a greater burden than he cared to think of.

Debts, debts, debt! he muttered. *I hate debt; I'm not going to borrow any more money. We shall all have to work harder, do more, take on some projects that will bring in some money.*

That thought made him feel better. *Yes! Projects! We must all work on things we haven't done for a long while.*

After his father died, with Ploy and Goy still at school, Samart and his mother had done what was necessary around the house and in the fields, but there hadn't been time for the extra things his father had done to make money.

"Charcoal!" he exclaimed out loud. "We know how to make charcoal, and this is the time of year to do it." They often made small amounts for their own use. "But why not larger quantities? Then we can go and sell it near the big road, where people can't make their own charcoal."

"Ploy," he called to his sister, as he marched towards the house with a determined step, "Where is Goy?"

"He's gone to swim in the river," she called back. "You didn't leave any instructions for him, so I said he could go."

"Swimming and playing," muttered Samart, as he came up the steps into the house. "That's all he thinks about."

"He's only a child," replied Ploy, defending her younger brother. "He needs to be with his friends sometimes." Her voice was calm and pleasant. She was good for Samart; she could often help him to relax when things got too much for him.

"All right," he said. "But from now on we are all going to work much harder." He shared with her what the monk had said, the turmoil of his own thinking, and then the constructive ideas that had come to him during the morning. "I'm going to start digging now; then we will all go to collect wood this afternoon."

Digging earth in a tropical country during the dry season is not child's play. But Samart was strong and fit; so by the time Goy came for his lunch, the pit was taking shape.

"What are you doing, big brother?"

"Digging a pit for us to make charcoal. After lunch, you and I will go to the rice mill to beg a couple of sacks of rice husks; then later this afternoon we'll all go up the mountain to collect logs."

"That should be fun!" exclaimed Goy.

Ignoring him, Samart continued, "Tomorrow we start - get the logs smouldering under the rice husks. Then, when the charcoal has cooled, you and I will go to BanNar village to sell it."

"How shall we get it to the main road?"

"We'll put it in those baskets Father used, and sling them on to a pole. I'll carry the load on my shoulder."

"Whew! Walk all the way to the main road!" Goy's idea of fun melted away. "Eight kilometres there and eight back!"

"There's no other way to travel this time of year; but we must do it. Otherwise our debts will mount up for the rest of our lives."

At lunchtime they took huge helpings of rice; they were very hungry and Ploy was a good cook.

"You enjoy rice, don't you, Goy?" commented Samart.

"I sure do," Goy answered with a quizzical grin on his face.

"Well, don't forget, if we can't pay this 150 baht to the doctor quickly we shall have to give him a whole sack of rice. And if our rice supply runs out before harvest, we have to eat that horrible root vegetable. And if this medicine is good for Lamon, we shall need more; so I hope we can all work hard on selling as much charcoal as possible before the rain starts. When the debt is paid off, we'll go on making and storing charcoal until the floods come; then we can take it in the boat, and get a better price for it in the rainy season."

Putting it like this made Ploy and Goy much more cooperative. They promised enthusiastically to help Samart all they could.

"We might even be able to pay back some of the money owing to uncle before long," he continued.

That evening Samart felt much better; at least they

were doing something. Even Lamon had been cooperative and drunk her medicine with only minimal coax-
ing.

The charcoal business turned out to be quite a success. They managed to pay for the medicine, and a
second supply as well.

Chapter 4
The secret is revealed

I t happened very suddenly during Lamon's second year at school: atrocious pain in both her arms, pain so dreadful that it made her cry and cream. This continued for days and nights, rarely easing. For a little girl, not yet ten years old, this kind of pain with sleepless nights soon took its toll both physically and emotionally. She became thin and pale, losing all her sparkle. And as for the others, anxiety and panic gripped their hearts.

To add to the troubles of the family, the rainy season had now started. The house leaked appallingly, and one night during a severe storm part of the roof blew off. The whole house was awash; there was nowhere to keep dry as the wind drove the rain into every corner.

"We haven't many nails and neither have our neighbours," announced Samart next morning. "I don't know when I can get the roof fixed properly. We must try to replace the tin today, Goy, but it won't be good. Another storm may blow it off again."

On these rainy nights the temperature dropped considerably. Usually they slept huddled together in a corner to keep warm. Blankets were unheard of; old sacks thrown out from the rice mill were the only covers they had.

"If you wish, I could take Lamon to the temple and the nuns will look after her," suggested the abbot. Knowing that his worst fears were confirmed, he frequently came to visit and console, and was concerned about the condition of the house.

"I prefer to have Lamon cared for here," was Samart's prompt reply.

The monk was puzzled at his attitude. Diminishing rice stocks, inadequate warm clothing and the house in such bad repair, yet Samart so quickly declined his generous offer! But if he felt hurt by the apparent rejection, he didn't show it. He simply continued to administer his home remedies, which seemed to ease the pain.

After many weeks, Lamon's pain did subside and she started to go to school again. She was delighted, as she enjoyed learning very much

But what was happening? When she picked up her pencil to write, and when she tried to turn over the pages in her notebook, things weren't the same as before. She could see that her fingers were holding the pencil, but she had no sensation in her hand. She couldn't feel how many pages she was turning over. Lamon was puzzled, but decided that it must be a result of all the pain.

"We are waiting for you, Lamon," called the teacher one morning in school. "Be quick and find the page."

Lamon said nothing, but grew confused and fumbled even more with her notebook, desperately trying to separate the pages. A friend eventually helped her.

"Please, teacher," came a timid voice from the class. "Please don't clean the blackboard yet, I haven't finished copying into my notebook."

Once again all eyes were on Lamon.

"Come along, Lamon, you must be quicker. Why are you so slow these days?" said the teacher abruptly. "I think if you haven't finished writing, you must copy from someone else later. We must get on with the lesson." With that blunt remark, he cleaned the blackboard.

Lamon was silent. Tears welled up in her eyes, ran down her pale cheeks and splashed onto the open book. After this had happened several times, she became very frightened and began to withdraw, losing all motivation to study.

Even though the teacher had seemed impatient with Lamon, he was concerned. She had previously been so quick and bright, often first to complete her writing. Now he watched her day after day struggling to control the pencil, always agitated when trying to turn over a page.

"There must be something radically wrong with Lamon's hands," he confided one day to the temple abbot, knowing he was friendly with the family. "I took a look at them today. Not only is there weakness and lack of sensation, but she can't straighten her fingers. As often as she pushes the fingers of one hand out straight with the other hand, they immediately curl over again."

"Are all her fingers affected?" the abbot enquired.

"Not quite all, I think, but several; she says all her fingers feel abnormal."

"Do you know what is wrong with Lamon?"

"I am very suspicious," the teacher said slowly. "I know what it looks like, but I don't want to mention the name of this disease. I can't understand why it should be found in a family like hers."

"I believe you are right," agreed the abbot, "I am sure it is that disease. And now she has so many symptoms, I'm afraid she will have to stop going to school."

The teacher reluctantly agreed.

"I see the family quite frequently," sighed the abbot. "I'll have to explain to Samart in more detail what it is, and what to expect in future."

The abbot's newly-shaven head shone in the morning sunlight as it hung down in despair. Approaching Lamon's home, his footsteps were slow and his heart so heavy that he wouldn't have minded dying on the way. It was obviously his duty to forbid Lamon to go to school any more. He knew that once the news of her disease became public around the village, some people would reject Lamon and perhaps the whole family. But he didn't see any point in warning them - they would find out soon enough.

As he had been hoping, the three teenagers and Lamon were all home. They were always delighted to see him, so they quickly gathered around as he sat cross-legged on the floor and began to chat with them.

Samart was well aware of the condition of Lamon's hands; he and Ploy had been examining her strangely-curling fingers every day. They were perplexed to see her in this condition, and very frustrated because there was nothing they could do for her.

The monk came to the point quickly. "I am now convinced what disease Lamon is suffering from. It is very difficult for me to have to explain to you, but it is necessary for you to know the details."

"Never mind, father," said Samart, addressing him with the intimacy which was commonplace between them these days. "Whatever you have to tell us, please tell us the whole truth. We've already guessed that this is a serious disease; it will be a relief to have the proper details, however bad they are."

"It's difficult to know what to call this disease," began their friend. "Some people call it the dog's disease because at some stages the skin becomes ulcerated and coarse, and in some cases body hair, including eyebrows, fall out."

"So it reminds you of a mangy dog, I suppose!" said Samart in horrified tones.

"I'm afraid you are right. And yet this doesn't happen to everyone," continued the monk, hastening to soften the blow. "For some, their hands get a little worse than Lamon's are now, and feet can be affected also, but that may be all. The deformities of hands and feet do not get better, but there are no more skin symptoms."

"Perhaps if we have a special merit-making ceremony soon, Buddha may prevent Lamon from getting any worse," ventured Ploy. She had lost faith in the only medicine available in their village, and "merit-making" was the only alternative she knew.

"Where shall we get the money?" enquired Goy bluntly. He was fed up with hearing about Lamon and her disease, and disgruntled about anything that diverted cash from their everyday needs.

"It's when the disease progresses to its worst extreme - when skin all over the body is affected and more deformities develop - that people begin to call this *Rook Khi Thut* - the disease of angel's droppings," the abbot kept to the point. "We Thai people hate and fear it. In its worst form we feel we can't find a name bad enough for it. Because we believe it is a result of evil in a previous existence and is controlled by the spirit world, a person with this disease is loathed and dreaded."

"You mean our little sister may one day become hated and feared in society." Samart spoke slowly as the truth of what was being said sunk into his mind.

"I'm sorry to say that could be so. However, this seems to be a very slowly-developing disease. Even if she does get worse, it will take quite a long time. And she may be one of the lucky ones - perhaps it will start to get better now."

They were all silent. In spite of his lack of firsthand medical knowledge, this monk had painted a remarkably accurate picture of the symptoms and progress of a disease dreaded not only in Thailand, but all over the world: LEPROSY. Though it hadn't been said they realized that all of them, not only Lamon, might be ostracized, once people in the village understood what was wrong with her.

Samart was the first to break silence. "Never mind," he said in a tone characteristic of his Thai Buddhist culture. "We can bear it. We'll protect her from people who despise her. I'm not afraid of this disease. She is my sister, and I love her and will care for her."

The abbot remained silent. These were brave words from the young man, much easier to blurt out than to live up to. And yet the monk knew that if anyone could keep his word, it was Samart.

"I need to tell you one more thing." It was easier for the abbot to continue, now that Samart's remark had broken the tension. "Lamon will have to stop going to school. I've discussed it with the teacher, and we feel it is the only thing we can do. For the sake of Lamon herself, and the other children and their families."

"Hooray," shouted Lamon, standing up and dancing

around. "I hate school when I can't write properly. I'll stay at home and help with the work. And I can play with Goy."

She had listened to what her beloved "father" had said, but she couldn't really understand it or apply it to herself. She knew she had abnormal hands that were a nuisance for doing some jobs; but now all the pain was gone she felt fine and much stronger.

"Why aren't you at school today, Lamon?" asked one of the neighbours soon after the monk's visit.

"Something's wrong with my hands, I can't write very well. The Reverend Father says I should stay home."

"Are your arms still painful, then?"

"No, the pain is all gone, but now I can't straighten my fingers."

"Let me see your hands." The neighbour sounded as though she needed to be convinced that Lamon had legitimate reason for missing school.

Lamon was not embarrassed. "Look," she exclaimed as she held them out, "I can't turn over the pages of my notebook, and the pencil doesn't go where I want it to!"

"Pitiful," murmured the friendly woman. She stroked the little hands, gently pushing the fingers into a normal straight position, only to see them bend over again and again. "Let me look at your face," she continued uneasily.

"Aunty, I can still use my hands if I want to lift bigger things," Lamon assured her. "I can grip very tight. Just feel this!" Without further warning, she grasped the woman's arm with both hands and squeezed hard.

"Ouch!"

Lamon had made her point!

It didn't take long for the news to spread around the group of small hamlets. Almost immediately Uncle appeared.

"I hear Lamon has a skin disease, and something's wrong with her hands. Is this true?" he demanded.

Samart was reluctant to discuss her condition with anyone, but he realized he could not withhold information from his one close relative.

"I'll call her. You can see for yourself. Who told you about her?"

"I heard it from several people," Uncle replied. "So I went to ask the medicine man if he knew about her."

Samart's heart sank. He realized he wouldn't be able to hide anything from Uncle, or make light of Lamon's condition.

Lamon came running across the compound, to where they sat on a bench under the house. As she recognized her uncle, she stood still a few yards away from him, made a polite little curtsy and with head bowed, *wai*'d him respectfully.

Uncle acknowledged her with a nod. He did not show any reaction, but inwardly he felt sickened. Her action showed quite clearly her clumsy hands and crooked fingers. Her palms could not meet neatly, because her bent fingers got in the way. The rumours he had heard about her disease were confirmed.

"What other symptoms has she got?" he asked Samart.

"Not much," came the curt reply. Samart felt threatened, not knowing what his uncle's reaction to the disease would be.

Ploy had now joined them. She loosened Lamon's skirt at the waist so as to let Uncle see the lesions on the buttocks.

"We were very encouraged when Lamon had drunk

two lots of the doctor's herbal medicine." Samart seemed to be relaxing now and able to tell his uncle the whole story. "At first these were red and angry and puffy, but after the medicine they settled down. The inflammation disappeared and they've had this harmless white look ever since."

"And the other week when we were making charcoal," Goy now took up the story, "a piece of smouldering wood fell on to her foot. She said it didn't hurt, so she didn't take care of it. We could see it was a real burn but she insisted she had no pain. In the end it went septic and Ploy had to clean it up for her and put ointment on it. I remember when I burned my leg once, it was very sore, I didn't want anyone to touch it!"

They all smiled as he related the experience.

"Lamon never cried or complained when big sister did the dressings. It's better now, but look at the scar." Goy pointed to Lamon's foot and looked at his uncle.

"Sometimes red lumps appear here and there on the skin," Samart continued. "Lamon says they are painful if we press them, but they disappear after a few days. They come and go in different parts of her body all the time." Samart presumed they were yet another phase of the disease.

Uncle sat and listened to them all talking. "It's unbelievable, I don't understand it," he said. "My own niece with that disease. No one else in our family has ever had it. We always go to the temple and make merit, your father and mother were good people. It's very strange and frightening. Unthinkable what might happen to her in the end ..." He seemed about to ramble on.

"Don't tell us any more," Samart interrupted. In recent weeks people had filled his ears with horrifying stories about what leprosy patients can look like in the final stages. So far he had kept this to himself. He was still hoping and praying to Buddha that Lamon would get better.

Whatever Uncle felt and feared, he did not recoil or show a hostile attitude. He held and stroked her hands and offered his sympathy, and left in a good humour. Samart felt very relieved that his uncle knew the truth. Ever since the abbot warned against telling the relatives, Samart had never been to visit them. He had become embarrassed about the lack of communication, but never dared to go

"I wonder if Uncle might offer to put the money down for a merit-making ceremony," Samart confided to Ploy later.

"I'm sure he can't afford it," said Ploy, in a tone of voice that was making excuses for Uncle and his family. "They aren't very well off themselves, and we already owe them money for the funerals."

Samart didn't need to be reminded. "That's true," he retorted fiercely, "but one day we will repay him. I will not be dependent on anyone!"

Chapter 5
Moving On

By 1953, the year Lamon was ten, the family were at desperation point. After a series of bad harvests, their home-grown rice was not enough to last the year. They would have been willing to work for others in return for a wage, but everyone else was just as poor, and none had work to offer. The charcoal business provided some income, but with so many other families in the same plight there were more charcoal merchants, lower prices, less profit! So they frequently had to resort to eating the bitter root vegetables from the hills around to keep away the hunger pangs.

Lamon's disease was definitely getting worse. Samart's heart felt like lead each time he glanced at her hands; he hated now to pick them up. During the last few months it had become impossible to stroke the fingers out straight. Now the joints were becoming stiff and even the thumbs were affected. Her little ten-year-old's hands reminded him of a bird's claw.

Something quite drastic had also happened to one of her feet.

"When I walk, it feels as though my foot gets in the

way," she told Ploy one day. "I can't lift it up, the ankle joint doesn't seem to work any more." This dropped foot was to give her increasingly the characteristic leprosy gait.

Lamon wasn't exactly rejected by her friends; she just got left behind when they played running-about games. Or if they played cooking and made mud pies, she wasn't able to handle the mixing sticks and the makeshift containers properly. So Lamon herself gradually withdrew; she couldn't bear being left out.

"Goy, how would you like to go with your cousin to work in Singburi?" Samart asked his fifteen-year-old brother one day.

"Singburi?" Goy exclaimed, stunned. "But that's fifteen kilometres away. Where would we live?"

"Aunty's relatives live just on the outskirts of Singburi town. You can stay with them, then go each day into the town and hire yourselves out to carry goods from the wholesale market to the river wharf or bus stop or wherever people ask you to go."

"How do we know anyone will want to hire us?" Goy argued. "So many men are already doing this kind of work."

"Yes, that's true," said Samart cautiously. "But Aunty's relatives have a son who's been doing this kind of work with his friend. Now they have got better jobs, and if you start to work with them before they leave, you'll be accepted by the other carriers. They have a good big cart which you can use for moving big loads that can't be carried on your shoulders."

Relationships with Uncle and his family had improved considerably in recent weeks. Samart now felt free to visit their home and discuss his problems as often as he liked, and he had just returned from such a visit. He seemed to be in quite a lighthearted mood, but at the same time his "organizing" tone of voice was coming through. Goy sensed that he wasn't going to have much choice about going away to work.

"The wholesale market," repeated Goy thoughtfully. "What time would we have to start work then?" He knew about the middle-of-the-night activities that go on in fresh food markets.

"The sooner you are on the spot to start work, the more you will get," Samart told him. "You're young and strong - the harder you work, the more money you will make."

Samart had indeed made up his mind that Goy must go to find work in their neighbouring provincial town. Things were becoming increasingly difficult, and if Goy went away there would be one less mouth to feed. Goy could keep himself and might eventually be able to help the three at home.

"Yes, I'll go," said the fifteen year old finally, without too much enthusiasm but without having to be persuaded. "Sometimes I get fed up here. We're so poor and life in this village is very dull. Anywhere will be better than here."

Samart was well aware how disenchanted Goy was with village life, and that Lamon's sickness was a problem to her teenage brother. Goy tried not to grumble about her, but sometimes he lost control and blamed her for their difficult circumstances. He hated having so little rice to eat. Samart and Ploy never scolded him for his outbursts, because they understood how he felt. They were all prone to lose their temper at times. Much as Samart disliked breaking up their family, he realized it would be best for Goy to leave.

"You're lucky to have this opportunity to go and look for work," Samart told Goy next day as they walked along the path towards Uncle's house. "I really envy you, I often wish that I could get away too." As the words slipped out, Samart knew they were only partly true. At times he was so discouraged and despondent that he did consider leaving to find work himself. And yet something in him always came to the surface and brought back his determination to stay and care for his sisters.

"You may be conscripted into the army next year when you're 21," Goy said. "It isn't worth you going to look for work now, big brother."

"Yes, that's right," admitted Samart. "I dread to think what will happen if I do have to go. It's one thing to choose a place to work not far away. It's quite different to be forced to join the army or airforce and be sent far away, only able to get home occasionally."

"Perhaps your luck will change and you won't have to be conscripted," encouraged Goy as he realized how responsible Samart felt for their sisters. In his better moments he felt sorry for Lamon and realized that Samart and Ploy seemed trapped into caring for her. "What really happens at signing on day?" he asked Samart.

"First of all everyone has to have a medical check up," his brother explained. "I'm well and strong so I'm sure I'll get through on health grounds. But then it's like a lucky dip!" Samart chuckled as he thought about what others had told him.

"Everyone has to file through a room and fill in forms. Hanging overhead is a box, too high for anyone to see into. As the men pass under it, everyone has to reach up, feel inside the box and take out a card."

Goy listened with interest as Samart continued the story. "Inside the box are two colours of cards - black and red. If you pick out a black one you don't have to join up. If you get a red one you read the instructions printed on it which tell you whether you are in the army or the airforce. Finally you are told where you have to report and when."

"Being in the forces isn't all that bad," commented Goy. "For poor people like us it's quite good, at least you get a regular income. I hope I get a red card when it's my turn to sign on."

"That's right," agreed Samart. "I wouldn't mind at all if it weren't for our sisters."

"Never mind," said Goy. "I expect our luck as a family will change one day. It can't get much worse."

Goy enjoyed his visit to Uncle's family, and found his cousin was very enthusiastic about their proposed venture in Singburi. Plans were made, a departure date was decided, and Uncle said he would inform his wife's relatives when the boys would arrive.

Goy felt very excited as he walked home with his brother that evening. He knew it would be hard work, but he was going to be free and had a good chance of earning enough to keep himself. And he would be able to eat rice every day!

"Did you get a red card or a black one?" shouted Ploy as she ran to meet Samart. He had been away for two whole days and life was bleak without him around.

"A red one," he replied gloomily. "I have to join the army next week, and can't come home at all for the first three months."

"Three months!" she wailed. "What shall we do?"

Samart could only remain silent. For months he had been imagining his "signing-on day", but had still gone on hoping that he would get a black card. Now he had to leave his sisters alone. They would have to manage as best they could without him.

Samart was hot, tired and hungry. The thought of the inevitable boiled root for supper sunk him deeper into depression.

Eighteen-year-old Ploy had been taking hard knocks for years now. She seemed to be coping with them without trauma, rebellion, or even self-pity. But now, as they arrived home, all the pent-up anxiety and strain was let loose. She lay on the floor sobbing, her whole body shaking, unable to control herself. Finally, worn out, she slept fitfully for a few hours.

Lamon knew at once what had happened when she saw their faces. Seeing Ploy in such turmoil, she was terrified, and ran to her big brother for protection. He put his arms round her and held her firmly, as he had so often done before. In that moment she was calmed and comforted. She knew he was going away, she knew it would be difficult, but somehow she felt a new confidence and assurance that they would get through and that things would turn out for the best.

Army life wasn't bad, in fact there was much to commend it. Samart ate well, and his small financial allowance felt like a fortune in comparison with the "nothing" he had been used to. This sudden affluence made it all the harder for him when he thought of his sisters and the plight they were in. It was difficult to get food and other necessities to them regularly because his leave was infrequent, but he was ingenious enough to find a way.

"Ploy, Ploy!" rang out an excited voice from below the house one morning in the spring of 1955, about a year after Samart had joined the army.

"Come up into the house," called Ploy mechanically, knowing the customary invitation wasn't necessary for this good friend. "What's all the excitement about?" she asked as a beaming face appeared at the top of the steps.

"Yesterday my father went to a village council meeting, and the headman told them about a new project." The young woman stopped to take a breath, but quickly continued, "The idea is that a group of people from this village can volunteer to travel about transplanting rice seedlings during planting season."

"Nothing but transplanting rice seedlings all day and every day!" Ploy exclaimed, putting a damper on her friend's enthusiasm. "Just the thought of it makes me feel like wanting to die. Have you ever worked at transplanting rice for hours on end?"

"No," came the somewhat deflated reply.

"Well, you'll know what I mean after the first two hours, and after two days you may be ill. Anyone who survives the first week will have a chance to make a go of it. But it surely is hard work!"

"Ploy, don't be such a wet blanket! It's a chance to make money! We'll be well paid and able to have better food and other things we need. I thought you'd be pleased at the prospect."

"I know you'll make money, but I've done this kind of work before. You'll be paid so much for every quarter or half acre, and when you start you'll be very slow. Then think of the heat! At that time of year it's at least 120° F in the sun, and there's no shade in the middle of a paddy field. By the time you've been stooping forward for even half an hour you'll feel your back is breaking, you'll be nauseated, and when you try to stand up straight it will be torture."

"I think I'll go home," said her friend impatiently. "You're obviously against the idea so you won't consider going along with the group."

"Me!" exclaimed Ploy. "How can I go? I have to stay here to care for my sister."

"I meant to tell you that my granny says she'll keep an eye on Lamon so you can go with us. But if you're so afraid of hard work there's no point in bothering. I thought you and Lamon were more desperate for money than any of us, and would do anything in order to eat rice every day."

Ploy felt cut to the core at the accusation that she was afraid of hard work. Anger and confusion welled up, but she couldn't speak. Conflict raged inside her and, as self-pity got the upper hand, tears began to pour down her cheeks. She sat on the floor dejected and helpless.

"I can't go," she whispered, struggling to make her words audible. "Samart will be angry if I leave my sister." She felt like a stricken animal caught in a cage from which there was no escape.

Lamon was in rather a dejected mood, and at first had hardly listened to the conversation. Hearing her name had jolted her awake.

"Ploy, you must go," she coaxed. "We do like to eat rice every day, don't we? I think it's a wonderful idea, and I shall be very sad if you stay home for me. I'm twelve years old, and I can look after myself quite well now. If I do need help the grannies nearby will be good to me. Please go, Ploy, even though it will be hard work for you."

"I'm not afraid of the hard work," said Ploy. "I've transplanted rice before, I know I can do it even though it's exhausting. But I truly am afraid of our brother. If he comes home and finds me gone he'll be so furious that I can't imagine what he'll do."

"He won't be able to do anything to you," giggled Lamon. "I'll tell him that I persuaded you to go. Let him be angry. He'll calm down when I remind him how desperate we are for food. I'll make sure that he eats boiled root for supper when he comes!" she concluded with glee, looking eager for the confrontation.

They all laughed and the atmosphere relaxed.

"So there's hope that you will go along then, Ploy?" asked her friend with renewed enthusiasm.

"I'll think about it." Ploy was still reluctant. "Perhaps our brother will come home again before the working party leaves, then I can discuss it with him."

"That's very unlikely, he's only just been home," observed Lamon. "You must go, Ploy, you can't miss this opportunity."

Chapter 6
New insights for Samart

Samart did not return. With persuasion from friends and neighbours, and much pressure from Lamon, Ploy went along with those leaving the village to find work one morning in June.

The group had an air of excitement and enthusiasm, with great hope of profitable results. They were to walk out of the village to the main road where a specially hired truck would pick them up. Their destination was the district of Inburi, a rural area about twelve kilometres away as the crow flies, though they had to travel more than thirty kilometres to get there.

Men and women, young and old, all wore the "farmers' uniform" - thick long-sleeved shirts in navy blue or black cotton, fastening up to the neck. The men wore matching trousers, the older women matching sarongs. The younger women's brightly coloured sarongs made an attractive splash of colour. The straw hats which everyone wore were tattered and old.

Lamon didn't feel apprehensive about being left alone. She too was expectant, knowing that if the project worked out well it would benefit her as well as her sister. So she was among the enthusiastic wellwishers who gathered to see the workers depart.

In spite of her worsening condition, Lamon had plenty of friends, who didn't seem to notice her appearance. Everyone enjoyed her sense of humour, and her personality had become more important than her disfigurement. But now, most of these friends her own age had gone along with their families, not to contribute very much to the rice transplanting but simply for the fun of it.

The next few weeks were very lonely for Lamon, bereft both of her sister and most of her friends. But she was not depressed. She knew they would be back, bringing their wages in money and kind.

"Lamon, come to eat dinner at my house today," called one of the neighbouring grannies left behind to watch the houses in their compound.

As the days went by this invitation was frequently repeated. Lamon found herself well cared for and ate rice most days, which was better than her customary rations. She had no guilty conscience about eating in the neighbours' homes. She simply accepted the invitations and enjoyed the hospitality.

"Ploy, where are you?" Samart's voice rang out across the compound one hot, humid afternoon about three weeks after the working party had gone.

"Ploy! Lamon! Are you at home?" His baritone voice broke the sleepy silence a second time.

As Samart crossed the compound he noticed that a number of houses were closed up. Outside steps leading up to the living rooms had either been removed or covered with sheets of corrugated tin - indicating that the owners were away for an extended period. He was puzzled.

As he mounted the steps of his own house Lamon was just rousing herself from sleep. Her heart was pounding fast. A visit from Samart normally brought joy and delight - but this time it was different. To joke with Ploy and her friends about this confrontation was one thing, but the reality was very daunting. She as well as Ploy knew the furious abuse he was capable of.

"Ploy isn't here," Lamon blurted out immediately. His unexpected appearance gave her no time to collect her wits and deliver the calm speech she had been re-hearsing.

"Where has she gone? What time will she be back?"

"I don't know exactly. She will be away for a few more weeks." Lamon was fully awake now and, al-though still apprehensive, felt calmer and able to de-liver the facts without getting tongue-tied.

"A few more weeks! What do you mean?" queried Samart incredulously.

Out came the whole story. Lamon put great stress on Ploy's reluctance to join the workers, and finally told him of the massive pressure from friends, neighbours and herself that had eventually made Ploy give in.

Samart was so nonplussed that he didn't know what to say. He remained silent for many seconds as the implications gradually filtered through to his con-sciousness. Then he exploded.

"This will not do!" he shouted, his angry voice telling the neighbours that he was home and was reacting just as they had all anticipated. "I left Ploy here to care for you and to ensure independence for both of you. With Ploy gone away you are a burden to everyone around. You had no business to persuade Ploy to leave you alone like this. Our neighbours are poor, it is not right that you should be sponging on them."

"But the grannies are so kind, they said they really

want to help us," interrupted Lamon in self-defence.

"Of course they say they want to help you, they have no choice when Ploy leaves you alone like this. They feel sorry for you and probably they think they are making merit by giving you food every day. But in fact they must feel obligated to care for you. They can hardly cook and eat food before your eyes and not invite you to join them." He paused.

"But it was their idea in the first place," Lamon managed to get a word in. "Surely they wouldn't have insisted on Ploy going if they hadn't been genuinely concerned for us."

Samart stood up and began to shed his uniform.

"Go and take a bath," Lamon recommended, "then you will feel better. You must have a rest too. We don't have any rice in the house, so after your siesta you can go out to dig up some roots for our evening meal."

Samart said nothing, but her remarks registered. He busied himself pulling his dirty clothes out of his bag. Then he looked around the house and asked, "Where is the soap powder?"

"Soap powder!" Lamon exclaimed. "We don't possess such a thing, except for a few days when you are home. We don't even have a bar of soap!" She was taking every opportunity to remind him of their poverty, as she had hoped to do.

Samart did feel better after his bath, but he was still stewing inside with conflicting emotions. "I'm going to the temple," he called to Lamon as he finished hanging his washing out to dry. "I need to talk with the Reverend Father."

"Don't forget to collect some roots on your way back," Lamon prompted him. In fact, she presumed he had brought rice with him - he always did. But as he hadn't mentioned it so far, she had another opportunity to play her game of reminding him what their normal diet was. He was also playing a teasing game by deliberately waiting until the last minute before he produced the banquet for their supper! So although he was still annoyed with Ploy and all who had persuaded her to go, he went off in a lighter mood.

"Hello, Samart, I'm pleased to see you again," said the abbot as the young man approached. "I thought you would be over whenever you got home."

Samart saluted the monk with a *wai*, but quickly launched into a long speech of criticism about the people in the village who had allowed, even encouraged Ploy to leave Lamon alone. Finally he asked the abbot why he hadn't intervened and ordered Ploy to stay around to care for Lamon.

"I didn't see any reason why Ploy should stay home," the monk replied calmly. "Lamon is now almost thirteen years old and quite capable, in spite of her bad hands and her lameness, of looking after herself. She really has very little to do anyway."

"She has to go out and look for food and do the cooking. We've found that these are the jobs that make her injure herself. And her wounds just don't get better. So I've forbidden her to do any digging or to touch anything hot."

"Ah, but you don't understand," said the monk. "The neighbours who persuaded Ploy to go, also promised to care for Lamon and give her food."

This statement was like a red rag to a bull for Samart. Even though he was in conversation with a Buddhist monk, a man considerably older than himself, he quite lost control.

"Exactly!" he shouted. "That means my sister has become totally dependent on other people! I don't want our family to be sponging all the time. I sent Goy away to work and keep himself, and I have been forced to leave, so Ploy is the only person to care for our young sister."

"I'm sorry you think like this, Samart," said the monk, not in any way ruffled by the young man's outburst. "Buddhism teaches us to do good. You know the saying: 'do good, get good' don't you? Well, I suppose these grannies may have that in mind, but I don't think it's only that. They seem to have taken responsibility for your sister because they like her and respect you. They often speak about you with very high regard and admiration for the way you have coped with your family."

Samart tried to ignore this note of praise, he felt embarrassed by such talk. "I'm sure they do think much about the meritorious side of their actions," he said. "It seems ironical that they are still favoured enough to have rice in their homes and therefore are able to offer help to Lamon, thus piling up even more merit for themselves. But our family seems totally without merit, while desperately needing it. We continually have to be the recipients of other folks' good works, when what we want is the opportunity to do good ourselves."

"On the contrary," responded the abbot thoughtfully, "I feel that our teaching 'do good, get good' is working quite well for you at the moment. You have been trying to do good for all these years since your parents died. You've worked hard and been a good example to your brother and sisters. It seems to me that you are now beginning to reap your rewards - rewards that mean jobs and opportunity to earn money for three of your family. And then another bonus in these neighbours who are not only willing, and perhaps hoping for more merit, but who are taking real pleasure in caring for Lamon."

The monk paused to give Samart opportunity to comment. But he was too busy thinking these new ideas over. The fury inside him was subsiding. This kind of talk brought new insight into his understanding of Buddhism and was like balm to his tortured emotions. Once more he acknowledged to himself how much he appreciated this man, a person capable of observing circumstances and applying Buddhist philosophy to everyday life.

"Another thing you have to remember, Samart," went on the monk, "is this terrible disease of leprosy in your sister."

Samart was startled into exclaiming, "How can I forget? It's the source of all my problems."

The monk nodded. "But not only yours. Lamon's disease is the potential source of problems for the whole village, particularly your compound. Her condition is now so bad that all the adults, particularly the older folk, can have absolutely no doubt what is wrong with her. Therefore, if these grannies were acting according to Buddhist teaching they wouldn't have anything to do with Lamon or any of your family. They would be so sure that her previous existence had been vicious and evil that they would be disgusted with her. They would probably have turned all of you out of the village long ago." The abbot hesitated as though to allow his words to sink in. Samart was listening intently but said nothing.

"Under the circumstances, I can only conclude that we in this village, myself included, have virtually forgotten our Buddhist principles and let our sympathetic human nature take over. And then, what about the fear that is normally associated with leprosy? I believe your neighbours are so fond of Lamon that they would do anything for her. It's as though they don't even notice her poor, disfigured body. I myself marvel at their attitude because I don't see Lamon as often as I used to, but when I do see her I realize how bad she's become and it's rather a shock to me. I wouldn't be surprised if you don't feel the same yourself, seeing you get home so infrequently these days."

Another startled exclamation from Samart broke into what the abbot was saying. "It must be true," he said. "Perhaps that's why I dislike coming home these days."

"It could well be, son." The older man's heart went out to him. "Yes, these elderly people in your compound are a great example to us, and you need to be very thankful to them. I'm afraid you are wrong to criticize them for encouraging Ploy to go to work. It's the best thing that could have happened to Ploy. She's become an attractive young woman, and she badly needed to get out of this village and be relieved of her responsibilities for a while. I'll tell you now that if the group decide to go to work again for harvesting at the end of the year, I shall try to insist that Ploy goes with them."

By this time Samart's resistance was completely broken down. He felt he wanted to get back quickly in order to thank the neighbours for caring for his sister. He realized he hadn't even asked Lamon how she was, he had barely looked at her. He had done nothing but grumble and assert himself since his arrival. He felt ashamed, and knew he needed to get home to make amends.

"I too have often marvelled that the neighbours have not rejected Lamon," Samart told the monk, "when some have known for a long time what was wrong with her. Now that I understand many people think it is a contagious disease, I'm surprised that people were still willing to touch her hands and examine them closely."

"Yes," said the monk contemplatively, "it's an interesting question. I suppose the fear we have of leprosy is that we shall get it if we touch it or even come near it. But I think this fear only arises when it becomes severe and ugly. People seem to shy away from anything ugly, so perhaps we just presume that leprosy is contagious when we see infected wounds and chronic, smelly ulcers. I remember when I was a boy, before vaccination, there was an epidemic of smallpox in our village. Many people got it and died, it was obviously contagious. Leprosy isn't like that. Considering Lamon has had it for years, yet no one else has got it, I presume it isn't contagious. But who can tell?

"Those grannies in your compound have seen Lamon every day of her life, and the change in her appearance has been so gradual that they probably don't realize how bad she is. I suspect that if half a dozen people with severe leprosy were suddenly to appear in the village, then everyone would be horrified. There would be dread and fear and hatred, and the intruders would quickly be driven out."

Lamon was feeling somewhat aggravated when her brother reached home. He had been gone all afternoon and she was hungry. Investigation into his rucksack had given her grounds to believe there would be something better than roots for supper. However, because of his angry mood she had not taken the things out of his bag, nor started to prepare any food.

"Lamon," called Samart as he came up into the house. "Have you cooked the rice yet?"

"Rice?" she answered questioningly, trying to sound surprised. "I told you to bring some roots home because we haven't any rice."

"Little sister!" he exclaimed, "you know I always bring food home for us. Why haven't you looked in my bag?"

His tone was so gentle now, so different from when he left. She sighed with relief.

"Come on, let's get the things out," he continued. "Then I'll light the fire and you wash the rice."

Rice! she thought happily as she hastily measured out two generous helpings. Then she looked at what he had brought to go with the rice. There was pork fat which they would fry until it was crisp and then have lots of dripping for frying the other things. There was dried beef, garlic, eggs, and salty fish sauce for seasoning. What a feast!

Chapter 7
Lamon's hardest day

Late one afternoon, about two weeks after Samart's visit, sudden excitement brought the village alive. A group of teenage boys came flooding in.

"We're the advance party!" they announced. "The others are coming home tomorrow. Tonight they are staying at a temple in Singburi, in the morning they will do some shopping in the market, then a truck is going to bring them as near to the village as possible."

Everyone came tumbling out of their houses. Even the oldest grannies, who usually sat around in a drowsy state, came alive. The boys were bombarded with questions - how is my relative, how has the work gone, how much money have they earned?

I'd better get going and do some cleaning before Ploy returns, Lamon told herself. *What a good thing the boys came ahead to warn us!* She looked around the house, feeling embarrassed to admit that she hadn't washed the floor for days.

It was almost midday when the party arrived. If they were hot and tired, none of them showed it. Many of the young women had already donned their pretty new clothes, and all the adults were wearing new straw hats.

The arrival was like an avalanche - everyone talking at once, laughing and joking. Even before they reached their own homes, some were opening parcels to show off their purchases, which included watches and radios as well as food and other useful stores.

Lamon and Ploy greeted one another affectionately. "You look so attractive in that new blouse and sarong," Lamon told her sister admiringly. "I see you've had your hair done in a new style too."

"Yes, do you like it?" beamed Ploy.

"I think you look beautiful," was Lamon's warm praise, feeling very proud to have such an attractive sister.

Ploy had bought some new baskets and a shoulder pole, necessary to carry home all her purchases. As they reached the house, she set the baskets on the ground with a sigh of relief. At last both baskets were upstairs and Ploy began to unpack them. She removed a number of small parcels to reveal the mass of precious white treasure that almost filled both baskets.

"Oh, what a lot of rice!" Lamon exclaimed. "This will last for weeks and weeks!"

"I hope so," said Ploy, laughing as she saw her sister's delight. "There's thirty kilograms."

"Here's a present for you," Ploy continued as she handed one of the brown paper bags to Lamon. The young girl's face lit up as she unpacked the gift. It contained a dark red sarong and a pretty pink blouse. Both garments were made of cotton with nothing very special about them. But to Lamon they were very precious, because they were new and had been chosen especially for her.

However, as she bowed her head and raised her

hands to her chin in a formal *wai* - her way of saying "thank you" to Ploy - tears were spilling over and running down her cheeks.

What good are clothes like this to me! she was thinking. *I never go anywhere. I have no use for pretty, bright clothes.* There was no way to cover up this spoiled body or to acquire a pretty appearance.

The two girls were sitting on the floor facing each other. Ploy saw the tears but made no comment. Lamon leaned forward and put her head in Ploy's lap, her arms stretched out to embrace her sister. Ploy put her arms around Lamon's shoulders, and as she did so she realized how sweaty and sticky Lamon was.

"Are you ill?" Ploy asked her. "Your blouse is soaking, you must have a fever."

Lamon sat up and acknowledged, "I'm often like this these days. I often feel unwell, particularly when these hard lumps come up on my body."

Ploy didn't know what to say by way of sympathy, so she changed the subject. "Come on, let's cook rice and make some nice food to go with it. I'm hungry, aren't you?"

"Yes, I'm very hungry for rice!" Lamon brightened up quickly at the thought of a good meal. They were soon working together to light the fire. Lamon washed the rice ready for cooking and Ploy began to prepare the vegetables.

Lamon was delighted to have Ploy back, and suddenly realized how much she had missed her sister. She chattered nonstop about what had happened in the village during Ploy's absence and especially, of course, about the day Samart came home.

Life at home wasn't easy for Ploy after her working trip. Everything in the house and the village seemed drab and dreary, and she was constantly dogged by a sense of apprehension about Lamon. Her young sister's condition was worsening. Sometimes she felt repulsed by Lamon. She hated to admit it but it was true. So she was glad of excuses to be out of the house and spent a lot of time visiting friends. Occasionally friends came to visit Ploy at home but she didn't encourage them, finding it embarrassing to welcome them into the house with Lamon around. However, Ploy still loved her sister and tried hard to cover up these feelings. Some days her guilty conscience got the better of her, so she stayed home trying to be a companion to Lamon.

"Why haven't you gone to look for your friends?" asked Lamon one day.

"I'm concerned for my little sister," she replied truthfully. "I'm afraid you must be very lonely when I go away."

"Never mind," said Lamon, genuinely trying to seem indifferent. "When I'm unwell I like to sleep a lot, so it doesn't matter if you are away."

Secretly she was delighted when Ploy stayed around to keep her company. But she sensed that it was a duty for Ploy, so she urged her, "You're so much older than me, I know you like to have fun with the girls and boys your own age. Please don't stay home for me."

"If you really can bear to be on your own for longer periods, then perhaps you won't mind if I go away again at harvest time," ventured Ploy one day. "We're planning to have another workparty at the end of the year."

"Oh yes, do go," enthused Lamon bravely. "Then you'll earn a lot more money and we can have rice all the time."

Ploy laughed. "My dear little sister," she exclaimed, "rice must be all that you dream about."

"No, it isn't," responded Lamon in rather a hurt tone of voice. "I think about many things, but my ideas will never come to anything because of this disease. So at least if I have decent food it helps to cheer me up. Did you meet some nice boy friends when you were away?" Lamon changed the subject abruptly.

"Yes, we did," came the surprised reply. "How did you know?" Ploy's complexion had become a pretty shade of pink at the introduction of this subject. At nineteen years old she was definitely delighted by opportunities to be in the company of the opposite sex.

"I've seen you watching the boys here! I'm glad that I'm not interested in boys," said Lamon with a note of finality.

Ploy couldn't resist a little giggle. "I'm sure you'll soon begin to be interested in boys. You'll be thirteen at New Year time; all teenage girls like to have boy friends."

Lamon was quiet, and Ploy realized she had said the wrong thing. This younger sister, with her increasing disfigurement, would never be attractive to boys. There was an awkward silence.

"Perhaps it will be the easiest thing for me if I don't become interested in boys," Lamon commented in a matter-of-fact way.

Lamon's moods and reactions varied from day to day. Sometimes she was genuinely indifferent. Some days she was very depressed and miserable.

Ploy had two particularly close friends who often came to visit. Lamon loved it when they came. Even though she didn't join in their "adult" conversations, she thoroughly enjoyed listening in. Their chatter always centred around the people they had lived and worked with while they had been away. They were very excited as they anticipated another working trip at New Year.

Lamon frequently heard the name Jit, and soon realized these girl friends were sure that Jit had a special affection for Ploy.

"Do you like Jit?" Lamon ventured to ask Ploy one day when the friends had left.

"Yes, he's very nice," replied Ploy cautiously, but with obvious pleasure at the mention of his name.

"Is he good-looking?" asked Lamon with interest.

"Quite good-looking, though nothing out of the ordinary. What I like about him is that he's very kind. He asked me about my family so I explained that we're orphans. I told him about Samart and how concerned he is for us. Eventually I even told him about your illness and what it has meant. He was very sympathetic."

"Where does he live?"

"In Inburi district, about five kilometres south of Inburi town."

"Do his family own land?"

"Yes, some - enough to keep themselves in rice, but not much left over to sell. But they're better off than we are, because they live near the river and directly south of the new irrigation dam in Chainat province. I couldn't understand all he told me about the dam, but evidently when there's a threat of flooding, the authorities can close the water gates in Chainat and keep the river back. Then if more water is needed for irrigating the paddy fields, they allow a controlled amount to flow through."

"How long did he study at school?" Lamon persisted in questioning her sister.

"He was more fortunate than we were. He was able to stay at school and complete grade six. I think he's quite clever really, he seems to be very artistic ... says he doesn't want to be a farmer, though he can't see what else he can do. His parents have no money for more education and there isn't any other kind of work where he lives."

"Will you see him again when you go to help with harvesting?"

"Yes I think so, I do hope so," Ploy answered in a very nostalgic tone of voice and a dreamy, faraway look in her eyes. "He isn't like most of the other fellows, he isn't joking and frivolous all the time, he's quiet and thoughtful. He first noticed me one day when I was feeling rather depressed, wondering how you were managing and worrying about what Samart would do when he found out I'd left. I didn't feel like sharing in all the joking and laughter. So he came over to chat with me, and after that we often talked together."

As the harvest season approached, Ploy did not have to be persuaded to join the work party. She had found it very hard to settle down in the village. Lamon was well aware that she was becoming a great burden to her family - not that they ever said anything.

Lamon was pleased that Ploy had confided in her about the boy friend, but it underlined further the thoughts that kept going through her mind: What would happen to her when Samart and Ploy were ready to be married?

The day that Ploy left for the second time was the hardest day that Lamon had ever known in her life. She managed to put on a brave face as the party was leaving the village, joining the group of stay-at-home wellwishers as they gathered to wave goodbye. But her heart was breaking, and instead of staying around to chat she quickly went home.

Once inside her own four walls she gave in to her feelings. Tears overflowed as she sat alone and stared around at the sparsely furnished room and the nearly bare walls. At the sight of two prominent photographs of her parents, anger and resentment welled up inside her.

Her mother she had known and loved, but Father was remote and vague. She hadn't really missed him as Samart had cared for her and taken his place in the home. Today, however, as she stared up at the photos, she became acutely aware that life would have been different if they had still been alive. Their presence would not have prevented her illness, of course, but they should have been there to love and care for her, to protect her from this devastating loneliness and the indescribable bleakness of the future.

Suddenly she found herself speaking out in loud, angry tones, cursing and swearing in a way she had never done before. Angry with everyone and everything, she seemed to have forgotten the Buddhist philosophy about ill-fate and lack of merit, and the theory of just punishment for evil deeds committed during a previous existence. Such teaching was irrelevant to her situation. She was only conscious that there must be some controlling power somewhere - a power that had prematurely taken away her parents and was now causing her precious brother and sister to recede into worlds of their own. It was against this unknown, unjust controlling power that her attack was directed.

She rose to her feet and stomped around the room; she picked up the few unimportant items that lay around and furiously threw them to the furthest corners. Crossing over to the small shabby cupboard, she noticed the blouse and sarong which she had still never worn.

"What good are these to me?" she shouted, her anger mounting as she tugged at the cloth in an attempt to rip the garments to pieces. The material was good quality and still new, so it did not give way to her weak and trembling hands. She threw the clothes to the floor in disgust and peered again into the cupboard, as though deliberately feeding her fury. Seeing Ploy's pretty blouses and sarongs she flung them to the floor.

"She is beautiful. Soon she will have a husband. Let her take these things away and leave me to die."

Three shelves held all the decent possessions that the family owned. As she swept the cupboard bare, the only things remaining were her own brush and comb and a piece of broken mirror. These she picked up, and marched towards the entrance where the light was better. She sat down at the top of the steps and peered into the mirror. The apparition that met her gaze only added to her distress. As she stared at her own reflection the fury, the hatred, the jealousy began to fade. A sense of utter dismay and hopelessness overwhelmed her and plunged her into an abyss of depression and self-pity.

"Hideous! With this strange, abnormal skin, I look like the old women left behind with me in this village."

As she held the mirror up before her face, she couldn't help but see her own hands, now gnarled and ulcerated.

"And what good are these?" she asked as the ugly extremities glared back at her. "Revolting, useless!" she answered herself as she flung the mirror away.

She rose again, by now utterly exhausted, and staggered to a dark corner of the room. She collapsed and lay on the floor, crying and sobbing for a long time, totally uncontrolled. Her mind went back to some of the conversations she had recently had with Ploy: "Yes I do think a lot about rice, good food helps to cheer me up. Any other hopes and ideas I have will never come to anything ..." She remembered saying that when she had felt hurt because of Ploy's teasing.

"If I have to stay here on my own when Ploy and Samart get married," she continued talking to herself, "I shall often be without rice. Goy rarely comes home these days, and one day he'll get married, too. Samart is right, the neighbours won't take care of me for ever...

"It will be easier if I never do get interested in boys," her mind suddenly switched tack. "Obviously I shall never be attractive to them, I shall never be able to get married.

"I'm sure I am going to be a terrible burden to my brothers and sister when they get married. I suppose I'm an embarrassment to Ploy already. I must be or she wouldn't tell me to stay indoors so often when her boy friends are anywhere near our house."

The tension that had been brewing in her heart for several weeks now came to a climax. Increasing uncertainty about the future, leading to insecurity and fear. FEAR, FEAR, FEAR!

This hopeless situation could only get worse. There was no release, no cure. A disease that does not kill, but brings endless torment for a whole lifetime. There was nothing left to live for.

"Father help me. Mother help me." Perhaps the spirits of her parents might be nearby.

"I'm so frightened," she whispered. "Please, Lord Buddha, have pity on me. Please let me die."

Lamon eventually became drowsy and slept. She slept for many hours.

As she awoke and looked around the house, she was quickly reminded of her outburst during the morning. Things were still strewn around the floor. The clothes she had flung from the cupboard remained as they had fallen. She felt ashamed, and quickly went around picking things up and putting the room to rights.

As she peered out of the window she saw that the sun was well down in the west. *It must be about five o'clock,* she thought, *I've slept all day. I'd better hurry and take a bath before supper time.*

Samart had made arrangements with the neighbours to care for Lamon while Ploy was away. He had brought a large quantity of rice which his sister would contribute to the families where she was to eat regularly. In his usual businesslike manner he had explained to the whole compound that Lamon was not to do any cooking or touch anything hot.

So that evening, as Lamon took her cool, refreshing bath, her heart was at ease. She felt quite hungry, but she was assured of a meal. She didn't have to wait and see if anyone invited her, it was already decided whose home she would eat in each day. She thought of her brother with affection and gratitude, knowing that he did still love her and was very concerned for her.

Chapter 8
Lamon finds a solution

"**B**ut I can't get married," insisted Samart, trying to be patient. "I've already told you that I'm very poor, with no father or mother, and I have to take responsibility for my two younger sisters for a few more years."

"My daughter is very attractive," Mr Chalard continued, apparently undisturbed by Samart's outburst. "She'll make a good wife for you, she can cook very well."

"Yes, I know that Keng is attractive, I'm fond of her already. But I have no money to pay the bride price. I can't get married to anyone yet." Samart thought that this talk of no money would surely shut him up!

Not so. This honesty and integrity only made Mr Chalard more determined to have Samart for his son-in-law. "The bride price needn't be too high," he emphasized. "You can get engaged this year, then if you save up and finally borrow some money you will have sufficient for the marriage next year."

Samart was feeling irritated. He was more than mildly attracted to Keng - he wanted to marry her very much. But visions of Lamon in her wretched condition never left his mind. He knew without doubt that Keng would react badly to his sister. She would be totally unable to accept Lamon.

"I've already told you that my young sister has leprosy," Samart said, in exasperation. "Do you understand what leprosy is?" Not waiting for an answer, he burst out, "*Rook Khi Thut!*" - letting it be known without doubt that this was leprosy in its worst form. He went on to tell this insistent matchmaker that whenever he got married, he would want to set up his own home and take Lamon to live nearby.

A look of mild surprise passed over Mr Chalard's face at such a suggestion, but he recovered quickly. Samart was only succeeding in piling even more merit on himself in the eyes of this shrewd middle-aged man. Surely a young man with such high ideals would be worth his weight in gold as a son-in-law.

"You can build a small house for your sister on our compound," he offered. "You and Keng will live in part of our family house."

This was the last thing that Samart really wanted. He was silent, uncertain how to answer this generous offer.

For a moment Samart forgot how Lamon felt; forgot that she needed her own village as a hideaway, where she felt secure among people who had known her all her life and so could accept her.

Samart's mind was in confusion. Deep down he knew he should continue to say no. But not so deep down, he knew that his feelings of affection for Keng increased every time he saw her. He suddenly felt very flattered that anyone should be so keen to have him as a son-in-law.

A picture of Ploy's pretty face flashed into his mind and he chuckled inwardly, knowing that it wouldn't be long before some young man asked to marry her. So he would soon be relieved of responsibility for one of his sisters.

Could he really get married in another year's time? It would only be possible if adequate provision were made for Lamon.

Lamon, yes Lamon! She had been like a chain binding him for all these years, and yet only recently had he been tempted to think of her like that. As her name came into his mind he was ashamed of himself.

Lamon! Getting more hideous every day. Now her ears were getting enlarged, her face taking on the typical appearance of the atrocious disease. Her skin continually erupting in blisters which broke down to send out streams of serum and pus, leaving the body covered in scabs that took days to heal. Her hands locked in a claw-like position, quite useless. And because of the never-ending instinct to try and be useful, wretched ulcers were now a permanent feature of her feet.

Anger flooded Samart's heart. What right had this man to blithely offer a strip of his compound for a house for Lamon? How could he presume that his relatives and neighbours would allow such a thing? This was something to offer for the time being, but to withdraw later just as irresponsibly. Samart realized how near he had come to betraying his young sister. Even though he hated her disease, he still loved her and admired her attitude to life. On impulse he offered a challenge.

"If I am to marry your daughter," he said, "you and your wife and Keng must go out to my village to see Lamon for yourselves. You may understand better just how poor we are when you see the conditions in which my sisters live.

"It takes all my wages," Samart continued, "and

what Ploy can earn, to keep the three of us in food and clothes and repairs to the house. Also I frequently pay out money to temples and Buddhist projects in the hope that Buddha will someday heal Lamon when we have accumulated a lot of merit. It will take a long time to save enough money to get married," he concluded as he stood up to leave.

To his utter amazement and dismay, Samart received a message from Mr Chalard a few days later. He and his family would like to visit Lamon as soon as Samart could arrange it. *Horrors!* he thought as the reality of the situation became clear to him. *This could be the end. When Keng sees Lamon and the poverty of our village she could well refuse to marry me!* He felt wretched. *If only they could be patient, wait my time, do things my way. Why did I make such a rash suggestion?* However, there was no going back. If he refused to take Mr Chalard and his family out to the village he would lose face. No, he must keep his word and go ahead with what he proposed.

But how to proceed? Samart knew that his sisters would be angry with him if he turned up unannounced with the visitors. But if he went to warn them first they would probably be angry anyway, and perhaps tell him not to bring the family. Or Lamon might decide to hide away and not allow them to see her. He was in agony as he began to imagine Lamon's reaction to the idea of leaving the village and going to live in a strange compound with people who didn't know her. In his heart he knew that this would not work.

What a fool I've been, he concluded. *There's no alternative, I'll simply have to go home and tell them all about it.*

His sisters listened patiently, not showing their feelings at all. When he had finished his story Lamon was the first to speak.

"Well, it's high time you were married," she told him. "I've been wondering for some time why you haven't taken a wife. You are good-looking and capable in many ways. I'm sure you have no difficulty in finding nice girl friends. I've been concerned that you were delaying marriage because of me so I'm very relieved to hear that at last you have found someone suitable."

Samart was stunned. He had always thought of Lamon as his baby sister, yet here she was at fourteen years old talking like a mother or elder sister.

"This is the chance of a lifetime," her harangue continued. "If Mr Chalard wants you for a son-in-law so badly, and if they are so much better off than we are, I can't understand why you are hesitating. You must go ahead with this marriage as soon as possible."

"But what about money?" Samart asked. "I can't afford the bride price, even though Chalard says he won't put it very high. And I refuse to go into debt."

"Perhaps we could mortgage our fields to Uncle or one of your friends," suggested Ploy. "I've heard of other people doing that. Now that you've decided to become a regular in the army, and Goy has moved away, we're not likely to use these fields for rice planting ourselves anymore."

"And then if Ploy gets married before much longer you may have a bit of profit from her bride price. Then you could pay off the mortgage before it accumulates too much interest." Lamon spoke as though this was the final word.

Samart thought over these suggestions for a few moments, and decided they were reasonable.

"But it may be a long time before Ploy gets married,"

he retorted, playing for time and still wondering how to mention his biggest problem.

"Oh, but Ploy has got a boy friend already!" Lamon revealed this bit of information with great relish.

Samart raised his eyebrows in mild surprise.

"There's nothing certain about my friendship with Jit," said Ploy defensively. She was annoyed with her sister in case Samart was be angry that she hadn't told him earlier. But to her relief he seemed to overlook the statement.

Samart had already told his sisters what Mr Chalard had suggested about accommodation for Lamon. Now he was considering how to broach the subject again, feeling sure that Lamon would not be willing to go.

But Lamon was ready to play her last card. Since that terrible, unforgettable day more than a year earlier, she had done a lot of thinking. She had also visited the temple frequently and had numerous conversations with the abbot. She really loved the Reverend Father and was full of confidence in him.

"You don't need to worry about me," she said without emotion. "Whenever you two get married and leave home for good, I shall become a Buddhist nun and go to live at the temple."

The abbot had suggested this to Samart several times, but he had never considered it seriously. For one thing he wanted to keep their home going, and also he feared that the abbot wouldn't be able to honour his proposal. "I doubt that such a thing can happen," he told Lamon. "The Buddhist religion forbids anyone with your disease to enter a temple, so how can you possibly go to live there?"

"The Reverend Father told me that in theory that's true. But he says that in fact, it's up to him as the head monk to decide who will be admitted to the temple."

"I think he may have trouble with the other nuns and monks," argued Samart. "They may be afraid of your disease and unable to accept you. If the abbot allows you to live there in spite of their objections, it could be very difficult for you, and for him too."

"I know most of the permanent temple staff already and they are willing to talk to me, they don't seem to object to me," said Lamon with finality.

"Well, if you're so determined I hope it works out," said Samart doubtfully. "As Ploy is not going to be married immediately there's no need to make any hasty decisions."

They were both silent for a few moments. Lamon satisfied that she had made her point, Samart relieved that yet another of his problems seemed to have melted away.

"So you really are going to be married at last," Lamon broke the silence. "I'm so pleased for you. You need someone to care for you, you deserve a very good wife." Then she changed the subject abruptly. "Well, we need to start making plans and preparations for your marriage. You must apply for special leave from the army so that you can become a monk for three months during the next Buddhist lent season. You know you can't get married until you have been through that experience, it will make you into a true Thai man."

Samart was somewhat nonplussed to hear these seemingly adult suggestions coming from a young teenager.

"We must try to economize with what money we have," she continued. "Perhaps Ploy and I could start making charcoal again. We could store it up and then when you or Goy come home you could take it and sell it for us."

Samart didn't feel enthusiastic about that, but he kept quiet.

"Tell us what day you will bring Mr Chalard and his family, we want to get the house cleaned and have everything looking as nice as possible." Lamon's suggestions flowed nonstop, she was so excited.

"And at last I shall have a good reason to wear my newest blouse and sarong. Don't worry, big brother," Lamon continued affectionately, "you won't need to be embarrassed about our poverty, or about me. If it is a day when I have lots of these horrid lumps and bumps, or if my skin is bad with eruptions, I'll take a bath midmorning and cover myself with talcum powder, and after the introductions I'll keep out of the way so they won't have to see much of me.

"Ploy's friends can come to help prepare food for the visitors. I know they'll be pleased to help and they can make good food. They'll be glad of an excuse to be around and see your girl friend! That's true isn't it, big sister?"

"Yes," replied Ploy, half mesmerized. "Yes, I'm sure they will be pleased to come and help to make a meal." Thus jerked back into reality, Ploy herself had ideas to offer. Soon the three of them were chattering and planning with excited anticipation.

As Samart eventually left to return to his army barracks, he felt like a different person. It was unbelievable that his "little sister" had anticipated all this. Now he knew that he needn't be ashamed of his home and poverty, not even of his disfigured sister. Rather, he felt sure he would be proud of them on the day he planned to bring his prospective in-laws.

PART II

Chapter 9

Introducing Tawat

1945. World War II was over and Japan defeated. Theoretically, soldiers from many countries who had formed a united eastern army, and ended up in Thailand under Japanese domination, could now go home. However some of them found Thailand attractive and didn't want to leave.

One such young man was a Vietnamese. He had married a young woman from a mixed Thai/Lao family in east Thailand, and hoped he would find her still waiting for him. At the end of the war he was in a Thai army camp in Saraburi province. He received permission to stay in Thailand, was allowed to retain his rank and officially became a member of the Thai army. At the earliest moment he travelled east to look for his wife and sons, and they moved to live with him in Saraburi, where a girl was later born.

The family lived in Saraburi for four years, but they were difficult years for the wife. She was always homesick, finding the dialect difficult to understand and the food expensive and unfamiliar. She began to lose any sense of responsibility for the family, and seemed not to care if the children misbehaved. When her husband was at work, she would sit around crying for hours at a time, thinking about her parents and her home in east Thailand. The worse she became, the more her husband went out drinking. They quarrelled more and more frequently.

One day, soon after the younger boy had started school, the two boys arrived home to find Mother out. This was very unusual, but they didn't think too much about it. They helped themselves to the cooked rice and curry on the stove and went out to roam the streets and play with their friends.

After dark when they eventually came home, they found Father in a desperate mood.

"Your mother has left us," he said.

The boys stared at him in disbelief. "Where has she gone?" the older boy asked.

"I don't know, but she's taken your sister, and all the money that was in the house. Her clothes aren't in the cupboard either. She must have gone home to your grandparents, she can't stand it here."

In spite of the rows and bitterness, this man still felt real affection for his wife, and he loved his daughter. He had never imagined that she might leave her family. He was severely hurt and shocked.

At the earliest opportunity he went to east Thailand to find her. But try as he would to coax her back to Saraburi, she would not go. Her parents offered to have the boys come to live with them, although they were very poor. But their father couldn't bear to let them go.

With Mother gone, and Father often drunk and increasingly erratic in disciplining his children, they were left to please themselves. The younger boy, Tawat, had little interest in school and his attendance was spasmodic. He did learn to read and write and add up figures, but he preferred to play around the streets, often involved in deliberate mischief and vandalism.

By the time he was twelve years old, Tawat had completed his four years of compulsory education. Father and teachers alike realized that with his present attitude to life, there was no point in forcing him to continue at school, even if his father had been able to afford it.

Now Tawat had even more time to himself. His rebellion increased, his undisciplined habits grew. He became a nuisance, and even a threat to the community. Fortunately for Tawat, complaints about his behaviour went only to his father, not to the police. But the complaints came thick and fast, making Father very anxious. He realized that something must be done.

Despite his own apparent indifference to life since his wife left him, and his increasing bad habits, Tawat's father had maintained his link with the Buddhist temple. He had not given food to the monks when they came round the district morning by morning, nor had he visited the temple frequently. But he believed that people needed religion and so had made offerings at the temple occasionally on special Buddhist festival days.

Suddenly one day, father told Tawat that he was to go and live in the temple as a Buddhist novice.

Up at five am, the monks and novices were busy with their preparations for the routine daily tour of the village. Tawat had no choice about joining this procession. As a boy with a shaven head and wearing a saffron[1] robe, it was the only means of ensuring that he would have food for the two meals officially allowed to

---

[1] a bright yellow-orange colour

all Buddhist clergy each day. He obediently went along without question.

The file of shaven-headed monks in their saffron-coloured robes, carrying their large black rice bowls, is a characteristic sight throughout Thailand at daybreak. They process slowly through the village, ready to receive offerings from the people. Thai Buddhists go to a lot of trouble to ensure that freshly prepared food is ready for the monks. Women regularly start their days at 4 am by cooking rice, chopping up vegetables, preparing coconut milk to make rich curries and other delicious savouries to be eaten with the rice.

Preparation completed, the food is carried out of doors to await the arrival of the monks. It is often placed on a small table covered with a pretty cloth and decorated with flowers. Members of the household wait with the food, ready to make the offerings whenever the monks appear. Usually the women of the family actually make the offering, but sometimes the men join in the ritual also, and often the children are present - ensuring that they will know what to do as they grow older and take on this responsibility.

As the monks come into view they can be a very impressive sight, the rays of the rising sun striking down to exaggerate the already brightly coloured robes, giving a startling appearance of golden splendour among the dark trees and early morning shadows. As the procession moves slowly towards the waiting family, a surge of pride wells up in the hearts of the women who see their own sons taking part in this daily ceremony, making their contribution to the lifelong burden of "merit making". Many Thai people truly believe that this daily ritual is a necessary part of the Buddhist way of salvation.

The monks approach, the women take up their silver servers. The ebony bowls are tilted in expectancy towards the giver as she spoons generous helpings of rice into the bowl of each individual monk and novice. Finally curries and savouries are collected in separate containers by temple assistants. When the distribution of food is completed the procession moves slowly away towards the next house. Her meritorious deed for the day now completed, the woman making the offering slips off her shoes and kneels on the ground in an act of reverent worship and prayerfulness. She is asking the spirit of the Lord Buddha to deliver from the bad episodes in this life and to give an abundance of good things as a reward for this daily offering.

For Tawat and his young novice friends, however, this daily routine was nothing more than an exercise to keep body and soul together!

The collection of offerings completed, the monks were soon back at the temple where Buddhist nuns and lay workers waited to receive the food. While this was being prepared for 7 am breakfast, the monks and novices had their first session of prayers.

Tawat's initial reaction to life in the temple was one of bewilderment. He didn't know anyone, the routine was very strange, the discipline extremely exacting, and these daily prayer times seemed to him irrelevant. *What do these words mean?* he thought that first morning as he sat cross-legged among the monks, wearing a very anxious look on his face. There was no book of written prayers to follow. He could only sit and listen to the chanting of endless meaningless liturgy. *If these are prayers,* he asked himself, *what use are they to me? I can't understand all this chanting in a foreign language!*

He tried to listen and look attentive for the first few minutes, but his concentration span was very short. *It's all rubbish!* he muttered beneath his breath and promptly lapsed into a thoughtful daydream.

He was remembering his father and the situation at home. He wondered where his mother was. Then he considered the previous day's activities - the brief initiation ceremony when monks had come to his home, shaved his head, gave him his novitiate robes and chanted. Finally he was taken to the temple at about 4 pm, and his father left him behind in the care of the abbot. It didn't take this thirteen year old long to become acquainted with the other teenage novices. He found that two others were also there because of problems at home and because parents found them rebellious and uncontrollable.

"Why are you here?" he asked three others about his own age.

"I'm an orphan," one of them answered. "My mother died when my sister was born. Later my dad fell in love with another woman, but she was already married. Her husband got mad and killed my dad. I've lived with various aunts and uncles, but they all have too many children of their own. They don't want me. So my grandmother, who looks after my sister, sent me here."

"We are twins," said the other two bystanders, looking at each other with big grins on their faces.

"Yes, I can see that!" Tawat grinned back at them.

"Our family is very poor, we have seven other brothers and sisters. Our parents couldn't afford to feed so many, so they sent us here two years ago. We like each other and we do everything together, so we haven't been lonely. We rather like it here, much better than our home where we were often very hungry."

"Aren't you ever hungry here, then?" asked Tawat doubtfully.

"No," they all answered, "we get good food."

"Well, what about the night time? I've heard that monks and novices aren't allowed to eat after midday."

They all laughed at his apprehension about having to miss his evening meal.

"I always eat more at supper time than any other meal," Tawat continued. "Today I tried to eat extra at lunch time because I knew I was coming to live here. But now I'm beginning to feel hungry again. I don't know what I'm going to do if I can't eat until morning."

They all laughed again. "You'll get used to it," they assured him. "We were all the same when we first came, but after about three days you won't feel hungry and by the time you've been here for a week, you'll forget about suppers."

The previous evening he had laughed with them, supposing that if they could stick it, he would manage it too. But now as he sat musing during this religious assembly on a pleasant sunny morning, seeds of rebellion were threatening in his heart. He felt like an alien, and wished he could run away. Fortunately he had enough sense to realize that he had nowhere to go. If he went home his father would be angry and bring him back, so he might as well put his mind to it and stay. *For the time being at least*, he thought. *But who knows, perhaps I will find a way to escape and a place to hide eventually.*

He had completely switched off during that half hour. But now he was suddenly brought back to reality. The prayers were over, and his new friends were nudging him into action.

"It's breakfast time," they said. "We can eat!"

Tawat quickly joined the orderly procession of monks leading to the dining area.

It was indeed a generous and tasty meal!

After breakfast there were chores to be done and then school. The youngsters were taught simple historical facts about Buddhism, and also had to memorize words and verses that they didn't understand in order to be able to join in the chanting during prayer sessions. They were told that this was the ancient language of the Lord Buddha, called Sanskrit.

General subjects for novices included reading, writing, arithmetic and use of the abacus. Older monks who were illiterate or who wanted to improve their knowledge could also learn these. Every day was interspersed with sessions of meditation and prayers, the monks striving in their own strength to become perfect.

Gradually Tawat settled down and accepted the routine and discipline of temple life. Some days practical jobs both inside the temple and in the grounds needed doing. Tawat liked these days the best. He was always one of the first volunteers for items to be repaired, building walls or gardening.

Tawat stayed in the temple as a novice for four years, learning quite a lot about life as he observed the older monks around him. Some had genuine faith in Buddha and his teaching and tried to live up to Buddha's standards. Others were phonies, layabouts using the temple as a shelter because they couldn't get work or didn't want to work. Others were hiding from the law.

Even as a teenager Tawat began to form his ideas about life. He realized that if goodness and truth and right attitudes prevailed, then the world could be a decent place. But in his experience truth and faithfulness mostly did not prevail, goodness was not apparent and attitudes were likely to be hostile and hateful. Even in this religious environment he was surrounded by evil practices of various kinds. By the time Tawat was sixteen he was disillusioned with temple life and becoming restless again.

Buddhist monks are not confined to the temple all the time. They can sometimes visit home and friends, and if anyone gives them money they can spend it as they please. When Tawat was free he was able to visit his old haunts and associates in Saraburi town centre. One place he loved to go was a vehicle repair workshop. He became friendly with the owner of the shop, Mr Chooay, and enjoyed learning about vehicles and how to repair them. Even while wearing his saffron robe he was happy to squat down, peering underneath filthy trucks and inside the engines, sometimes helping to repair punctured tyres and other little jobs.

In spite of their difference in age, Tawat and the shop owner became good friends. One day when the two were chatting together, Tawat began to air his grievances and his increasing dissatisfaction with life in the temple. Suddenly, Mr Chooay offered Tawat a job if he wanted to leave the temple.

Tawat was excited and stimulated at this possibility. He had often wondered if and when he would ever be able to leave the temple. But if he had a job and promised his father that he would stick at it, perhaps he would be allowed to leave the monastic life.

Losing the security of the temple was actually quite a shock to Tawat. His father's place was not much of a home, and there were many temptations around him. Even though he had admired the genuine monks in the temple, and still desired goodness to be uppermost in his heart, yet once back in the world his behaviour deteriorated quickly.

However, he liked his work and stuck at it well. In spite of bad habits and moodiness there was a pleasant side to his personality. Mr Chooay liked him and he worked willingly, doing odd jobs and errands as well as learning about vehicles. Eventually he learned to drive.

Chapter 10
Tawat takes a risk

"**D**o you know anyone who would like a job driving a tractor?" asked a customer in the workshop one day.

"I don't think so," replied Mr Chooay, "but I will make enquiries, I may be able to find someone suitable."

The wealthy farmer from Nakhon Sawan province gave him more details. "The work will be in the district of Takhfa," he said. "Some areas where the tractor will be used are isolated, still forest land, with no one living there. We have trouble with bandits at times – they like to hide in the forests, so they aren't pleased when we clear these areas for land development. Life out there could be dangerous, but I'll pay good wages to anyone who is willing to work hard."

Tawat, overhearing this conversation, was beside himself with excitement. If only he could have this job! He was eighteen now, and since he had learned to drive he had often longed for a job where he could use this skill.

Conditions at home were still difficult and he only went there to sleep. *No one will care if I go to the wilds of Nakhon Sawan province,* he told himself. *Father will never miss me, I so rarely see him.*

During times of depression Tawat often preferred to go off on his own, and recently he had been thinking hard. Life seemed very unfair. He questioned what it was all about and why he had been born into such a situation. He had no answers. It would be good to get away from everyone and everything and make a fresh start - and where better than hidden away in the forests?

"I would like to volunteer to work for that farmer in Nakhon Sawan," ventured Tawat in the politest manner he knew, as soon as the farmer had left. Mr Chooay was rather taken by surprise at this sudden suggestion, but as he looked at the young man he saw an unusual earnestness. He knew that Tawat's life was full of problems, and realized in a flash what must be going on in his mind. Chooay had come to appreciate Tawat's keenness and reliability. He determined to give him a chance to make a fresh start and prove himself in a job that would bring more responsibility and more money.

Two days later, when the farmer returned to collect his tractor, Chooay said to him, "This young man has volunteered to take the job you are offering. He is trustworthy and I have no hesitation in recommending him to work for you."

The farmer looked at Tawat. "How old are you, young man?"

"Eighteen, sir."

"How long have you been driving?"

"About one year..."

"Hm. Not long. But you'll soon get the experience. Have you ever driven a tractor?"

Tawat's heart missed a beat, but he answered truthfully. "Not often, sir. I've only taken tractors out for short distances to test them when they've been repaired here."

"Not to worry," said the farmer. "If your boss here thinks you are capable of doing this work, then I'm sure you are. When can you start?"

"Any time, sir. When would you like me to?" Tawat glanced at Mr Chooay realizing that perhaps he should consult his boss, who had come to depend on him. But Mr Chooay was smiling, just as pleased as Tawat himself that such an opportunity had come.

"Tomorrow is fine," he said, meaning that Tawat could leave immediately without giving any notice.

"Oh, by the way, have you got a driving licence?" the farmer asked.

"A driving licence!" Tawat exclaimed. "No, I don't."

The farmer laughed at Tawat's crestfallen face. "Never mind," he said. "You won't need one for the tractor, but if you ever drive our truck you ought to have one. We can get it for you later. The police never come into the wilds of Takhfa, so you'll be OK when driving around our local area."

To leave in such haste posed no problem for Tawat. He had already warned his father, knowing that if his boss recommended him for the job he would probably get it. He only needed a cardboard box from the grocer's shop, to hold his few possessions. He could tear an old sarong into strips to tie up the box.

That evening he received his wages, which gave him enough for his bus fare, a bite to eat during his journey and some cigarettes. Hopefully there would be some left over for his needs during the next few days.

As Tawat said goodbye to Mr Chooay that evening he seemed like a different person. He had suddenly grown up and taken on an air of confidence never seen before. The older man knew that if circumstances were favourable, Tawat would make good in this new job.

Tawat knew that it had been raining most of the night and the thought passed through his mind that it might not be an easy journey. But nothing could dampen his enthusiasm today. He was excited beyond description. It didn't worry him in the least that he was shivering and his teeth chattering as he took his bath - pouring dipper after dipper of chilly river water over himself at four in the morning while it was still dark. This was his day, the beginning of life for him.

While waiting for the bus he looked down at his feet and saw that his decision not to buy new shoes had been right. Although he had washed these old ones in the river the previous evening, they were already wet through and coated with orange clay. He was regretting that he had chosen to wear his only decent pair of trousers, now splattered with the same orange design.

Eventually the bus came. Having already completed two tours of Saraburi market it now proceeded on its third and hopefully last drive over the same ground, to ensure that all who wanted to catch this early bus had a fair opportunity to do so.

The bus wasn't the most comfortable vehicle for rainy season travel, seeing there were no glass panes in its windows. Tawat managed to squeeze himself onto a small space on a seat near the front.

I'm glad I'm not sitting near the window, he thought. *The rain is bound to be driven inside the bus as we get up speed.*

The bus was packed to capacity, full of people and baskets inside, with larger baskets of livestock and vegetables perched rather insecurely on the roof. It left

Saraburi at about five o'clock, travelling towards Lopburi provincial city fifty kilometres away.

"Hey!" called out one of the passengers as the bus picked up speed and the rain became heavier, "Stop the bus and pull down the tarpaulins, we're getting wet!"

Obligingly the driver stopped the bus. Two agile bus boys climbed up to release the rather tattered semi-waterproof canvas which was attached to the roof. As the tarpaulines were unrolled, the passengers in the window seats held tightly to the bottom of them, hoping for protection against the wind and rain.

"Young man!" called the driver to one of the bus boys as he leaped from his perch on the window frame, "Come and clean the windscreen for me!" He handed a scruffy piece of rag to the teenager, who quickly sprang on to the front bumper and energetically polished the mud-splattered pane of glass.

The bus travelled steadily along for many kilometres, stopping often to take on still more passengers, who were now tightly packed down the centre and hanging out of the door. For passengers deeply embedded in the bus who wanted to alight before the terminus in Lopburi, there were only two alternatives. They either climbed out of the windows, or virtually crawled over their fellow passengers sitting in the aisle.

Tawat had been to Lopburi occasionally in the past, so he recognized the town when the bus stopped near the famous Monkey Temple - one of the sacred Hindu shrines in Lopburi province. As he stood on the pavement and took a quick glance around, he caught sight of another bus saying "Takhli". *That's it*, he muttered to himself. *I wonder when it leaves?* He couldn't see the driver around, and there weren't any passengers in it. He knew that the timetable was ruled far more by the number of passengers than by the clock.

Good, he thought. *Time to get some breakfast here.*

It was now after seven o'clock and still raining. He felt rather damp and chilly, so he was glad to see several food shops nearby. He ordered hot coffee and doughnuts, stirred lashings of sweetened condensed milk into the coffee and dunked his doughnut in it.

Lopburi was as far north as Tawat had ever been, so once the Takhli bus moved off he was on new ground. His instructions were to stay on this bus for about seventy kilometres, until they arrived at Takhfa, a market village in the southern part of Nakhon Sawan province. He had arranged to meet the farmer there about midday.

This bus was not so crowded, so Tawat could choose his seat and spread out comfortably. He soon fell asleep as the bus bounced and bumped over the never-ending orange gravel road full of potholes, some almost the width of the road.

It had stopped raining when he reached Takhfa, but there was still no sun. His new employer was waiting as promised, and as Tawat was quite ravenous by this time he was glad at the suggestion to go and eat rice. Rice with delicious peppery hot curry! He accepted a second plateful without hesitation, guessing correctly that this meal would be on his new friend the farmer.

This man, more than twenty years Tawat's senior, really did seem like a friend even though he was to be his employer. He treated Tawat as a fellow adult. Even though his clothes were obviously not his best outfit, he did look quite smart. His hair was tidy and he wore a felt hat rather than a straw one. In fact Tawat was soon to realize that his new boss, Mr Dee, was a wealthy landowner.

After the tasty meal they travelled by tractor into the wilds. At first there was quite a wide path, and the land around was already cleared.

"This is the area where we grow maize and cotton," Mr Dee told Tawat. "In a few years time when all the land is cleared, it will be very profitable."

The path got narrower, and the maize and cotton plantations gave way to a wilderness covered with scrub and wiry–looking bushes. Tawat knew he needed to watch how Dee handled the tractor through this rough land.

Suddenly, as they came over the top of a small hill, a clearing with a very nice-looking house appeared. Around it was a well-planned kitchen garden with peppers, herbs, and a variety of healthy-looking vege-tables.

"This is my house," said Mr Dee with an air of satisfaction.

So far so good, thought Tawat as he settled down to sleep that night, still at the home of Dee and his family. *Tomorrow I shall begin to find out what life is like roughing it in the wilds. I'm sure I shall be able to stick it without any trouble.* He relaxed and slept soundly until daylight.

Tawat adapted well to his new life. He enjoyed periods when he could be on his own with his tractor, and tinkering with tools. When he felt like company there were friendly groups of men who accepted him quickly. Tawat saw quite a lot of his boss, as Dee was often on the spot supervising his men and informing Tawat where the tractor was needed from day to day. The two men got on well together and seemed to like each other.

"We had a row at the house last night," Dee told Tawat one morning.

"What was it about?" Tawat asked, more for something to say than out of curiosity. He was surprised that his boss would confide in him about such matters.

"It was all to do with the land clearing project. Several of us have put our money together to hire workers and buy equipment. We've formed a Cooperative and I'm the chairman of the committee. I've had quite long experience in this kind of work, so I often speak up and offer my opinion. But last night some members were accusing me of taking too much authority and doing things my own way without consultation."

This was the beginning of a close and trusting relationship between Mr Dee and Tawat. As Dee told Tawat more about himself and his family, Tawat began to realize that it wasn't always so wonderful to be rich and influential. People often acted like friends but were really enemies, jealous people trying to make trouble.

As Dee got to know Tawat better, he felt concerned that Tawat had no decent home to go to. So from time to time he invited Tawat to his home, and he became almost one of the family.

Life had become very attractive for the young man. Not only was he able to visit Mr Dee's home as often as he liked, but in that home were his boss's daughters! One of them was about Tawat's age, and they soon grew very fond of each other. Eventually it became obvious to Dee that his daughter and Tawat were well matched. As he found Tawat trustworthy, hard working and a man with initiative, he was pleased to consent to their marriage. He also gave Tawat increasing responsibility, apparently preparing to accept him wholeheartedly as a member of the family.

Tawat enjoyed the added responsibility, but soon realized that it brought hostility from some of his

workmates. One or two of the men he had thought
were his friends began to show they were jealous of his
position. Even though he was very much in love with
Mr Dee's daughter and desperately wanted to marry
her, some days he wondered if he were foolish to go
ahead with this relationship. To become part of the
family meant that he was fast becoming part of the
machinery in the family business. He wasn't sure that
he wanted life to be always like this.

Chapter 11
Another chance for Buddhism

"I would like to apply for a period of leave," Tawat said to Mr Dee one day.

"Oh yes," responded his employer affably, "how long would you like?" Dee presumed that Tawat had decided to go home at last for a visit to his father.

"About one year," answered Tawat.

"One year!" repeated Dee with surprise. "What have you got in mind then?"

Tawat laughed nervously then continued, "I need time to think. I would like to go and be a Buddhist monk."

"You only need three months for that, surely."

"No, I would like to join the Order of Monks who live mostly out of doors, walking from town to town and sleeping in tents. For that I need longer."

"I didn't know you were so religious! Why do you want to join that Order?" asked Mr Dee incredulously. "You've already lived in the temple for four years as a novice. I would have thought you knew all there was to know about Buddhism."

Mr Dee and his family were totally irreligious. Living in such an isolated area with no Buddhist temples, they had nothing to remind them of religion.

"I think it's because I spent so long in the temple earlier that I want to go back now," Tawat said thoughtfully. "I want to get more acquainted with my religion as an adult, in the hope I can dislodge my childish image of Buddhism. By joining this different Order I hope to find men who have genuine faith in religion. I was very disillusioned as a boy in the temple."

Tawat had thought about all this a great deal before making his request. He knew it would be inconvenient for his boss. In less than two years he had soared from being a nobody to being the foreman and prospective manager. Sometimes he could scarcely believe that he had progressed so far so fast. Life now was so different from what he had known before. He couldn't explain exactly how he felt or why he wanted to go, he simply knew he must identify with his religion and find others who felt like he did.

"Well, I can't stop you if you are determined to go," said Mr Dee with resignation. "And if you really want to marry my daughter as I've promised you can, then I can't really sack you either!" Both men laughed.

"If you allow me to go, then to come back and continue working here, and eventually marry your daughter, then perhaps I shall be able to believe that I'm wanted in this world." Tawat was surprised at what he heard himself saying, and suddenly became anxious that Mr Dee wouldn't understand. "Please excuse me for speaking like this," he said in embarrassed tones.

"Never mind, son," his employer replied. "I'm pleased that you've mentioned it. I do like you, you've worked well for me, and I have confidence in you. I respect your feelings and I'm happy for you to go away for a while if it will help you. I hope you'll come back. The job will still be here for you."

The time spent as a monk passed very quickly for Tawat. Always on the move, constantly walking from town to town, he became very familiar with the geography of his country and enjoyed this outdoor life.

As he learned more of the deeper truths of Buddhism, however, he once again became disillusioned. Not with his fellow monks this time. Most of them seemed genuine in their pursuit of truth and perfection. Now he was disenchanted with the doctrine itself. He was learning about meditation and the "need to suppress one's feelings and emotions". But how was that possible? He had the image of his fiancee frequently in mind, and was also living and moving in very pleasant countryside. Trees, blossoms and beautiful birds surrounded him continually - he couldn't help but enjoy the scenery. But the teaching said he was not to observe these things, not to consider anything that was beautiful or attractive, in case it would lead him away from his pursuit of perfection and holiness. He was to erase these things from his imagination as quickly as possible.

Tawat finally came to see that if this was truly how life was supposed to be lived, the only way to find salvation and gain eternal life, then he could not make the grade. He must go back to his work and to the girl he loved.

All the family were pleased to have him back, and plans went ahead for the wedding. The date was fixed and the invitation cards printed. Tawat was very excited. As he looked back over his life, he could scarcely believe that this was happening to him. He had proved himself efficient and reliable, and now he was to marry into this comfortably well-off family. His luck had certainly changed.

His working conditions were improved also. During his absence several of his old mates had moved on, including the hostile ones. He now took over officially the job of manager for clearing Mr Dee's land, and as the owner's prospective son-in-law he was accepted without question.

Continually, however, Tawat was reminded that to be wealthy meant having enemies. As he lived in Mr Dee's household he observed "friends" coming and going on business, men who seemed without any kind of standard for their lives, men who drank too much and easily had rows with each other. Their business practices were often dishonest, and they were out to get all they could for themselves. Would he become like these men? Did he want to? He was already fond of drinking and easily went along with the group.

Tawat's excitement about his marriage and the sense of security brought by his acceptance by Mr Dee, sent him to dizzy heights of pride and self-satisfaction. He rejected all that he had learned as a Buddhist monk.

To this day it remains a mystery. Who fired the shot that changed Tawat's life?

It happened very suddenly and was over very quickly. Tawat was driving the tractor, with Dee sitting beside him. All at once there was a scuffling sound in the bushes, a man's face peering out, and then a shout.

"Quick!" cried Dee as he jumped from the still-moving tractor. But it was too late. Tawat wasn't able to act so quickly, and as he brought the tractor to a halt and tried to jump clear a shot rang out. His leg took the full blast and he landed in a crumpled heap on the ground. Dee immediately began firing back into the bushes, but without effect. As the attacker realized he had hit the wrong person, he made a quick getaway.

Tawat's leg was bleeding. He made an effort to stand up, but could not bear the pain. They stayed put for a few minutes to make sure there were no other raiders around, then eventually, with much help from Dee, Tawat managed to get up onto the tractor. Then he passed out. Dee drove Tawat back to the house.

Dee himself felt shocked and shaken by the incident, but he knew Tawat needed to be in hospital, and managed to get him into the landrover.

The question was, which hospital? The nearest was a government hospital in Chainat town, about eighty kilometres away. However, Dee had heard of another hospital in the village of Manorom, about 13 kilometres north of Chainat. This was run by foreigners, a Christian hospital with a good reputation. Suspecting Tawat's leg was severely injured, Dee decided to try and make it to Manorom.

Chapter 12
Life in the balance

"**O**nly a few more miles to go now," called Mr Dee. Tawat lay in the back of the land-rover, his whole body aching and tortured with weariness. The pain in his leg was indescribable as he wafted in and out of consciousness. The bumpy surface of the road didn't help. Most of the way it was just a gravel surface, though short stretches were sealed with tarmac where a village had paid for road improvements.

"What time is it?" Tawat asked shakily, noticing that it was now dark.

"After eight o'clock," was Mr Dee's half-hearted reply.

Both men were thinking similar thoughts. It was quite normal for a doctor to go off duty at 5 or 6 pm and not appear again before next morning. X-ray, pathology and pharmacy departments would probably be closed for the night too. So the two men were feeling despondent as Mr Dee drove through Chainat town, bypassing the government hospital there and starting the last lap of the journey to Manorom.

Yes, eight o'clock, muttered Dee to himself as Tawat lapsed into silence again. *Can the things I've heard about this Christian hospital really be true? A doctor available to examine seriously ill patients, path lab technicians willing to work during the night so blood transfusions can be given. X-ray functions for an emergency at any time, and even operations performed at any time in order to save lives...*

Mr Dee dared not share this kind of hearsay with Tawat. He could hardly believe that it would be true, but because he had heard firsthand from reliable sources that "The Christian" at Manorom was like this, he persevered.

He was still travelling north, but he knew it couldn't be far now. He had been told to look out for the signpost to Uthai and turn west there. After following a road for about a kilometre he would see the hospital off to his left. Literally in the middle of the paddy fields.

Yes, there it was! Through his rain splashed windscreen, the Uthai signpost suddenly sprang into view. And sure enough, as he turned towards Manorom village, he quickly caught sight of the bright lights off to his left.

That must be the hospital, Mr Dee thought, *with its own generator.* Decently lit buildings in a country village must be something important.

He now drove recklessly over the last few yards of gravel road and finally edged his way along the narrow path to the hospital compound. "We've arrived!" he announced as the landrover came to a stop in front of the nearest building.

As Mr Dee hurried inside he was relieved to find there were signs of life, even so late at night. The first person he saw was a young woman in a white uniform. *Oh, she's a foreigner,* he thought with sudden horror.

"Good evening," she said with a smile. "What can I do for you?"

Mr Dee relaxed as he realized she was speaking in his own language. "Shooting incident!" he exclaimed briefly as he moved outside again and went to open the back of his vehicle. "This young man has severe leg wounds and has lost a lot of blood."

As though the sound of their voices had set off a chain reaction, suddenly a whole group of people were coming to listen to his story. Two nurse aides in dark blue uniforms, the clerk from the reception desk, and two other men who had been sitting around chatting and seen the landrover arrive, all appeared. Dee was delighted to see that these were all Thai people.

"The shooting occurred this afternoon," he began. "We've travelled all the way from Takhfa. I couldn't drive very quickly because of the bad road and the rain. It's taken us four hours to get here." His speech came out in short erratic bursts.

They all peered into the vehicle as the missionary nurse shone her torch. It needed only a glance to confirm how seriously ill Tawat was.

"I think he could be dead already," murmured one of the men as he caught sight of Tawat's deathly white appearance.

Everyone went into action. The nurse quickly disappeared along the path towards the doctor's house. The nurse aides hurried to bring the trolley to wheel Tawat inside, and the two men helped lift him out of the vehicle onto the stretcher.

The clerk reached for his pad and started making notes. He asked the usual questions, about Tawat's name, address and age, which Dee answered without difficulty.

"Are you his father?" the clerk asked next.

"No, his father lives in Saraburi. I'm his employer and I don't know his family."

"Hm! That might complicate matters if he has to have an operation. It's supposed to be his nearest relative who signs the consent form for an anaesthetic."

"Well, I'm responsible for him these days. He's estranged from his father and never goes home to visit. He's going to be my son-in-law, so I think I could sign the form, couldn't I?"

The clerk grinned. "All right," he said, "sign here."

The nurse aides wheeled Tawat into the treatment room and had barely looked at his leg when the missionary nurse returned with the doctor. It didn't need an expert to assess that Tawat was critically ill, suffering from excessive blood loss, severe shock and serious leg wounds. Things were quickly set in motion: give intravenous fluid immediately, call the pathologist, inform the X-ray technician, give injections to relieve pain and shock and to combat infections ...

Mr Dee stood there bewildered. No one had any time to be concerned for him. He still found it almost unbelievable that all this efficient activity could be taking place so late at night.

Mr Dee was suddenly jerked back to reality as he realized the doctor was addressing him. "Are you his relative?" he repeated. The tall, placid Australian doctor need not have bothered about Mr Dee at all, but he had noticed the lone figure and realized that he looked all in. So he took time to listen to the whole story as it poured out freely.

"You must feel wretched yourself," said the doctor finally. "I'll give you a sleeping tablet which will help you to relax and have a good night's sleep. Now you need somewhere to stay for the night. Samrarn!" the doctor called to the helpful young man who had helped lift Tawat. "Could you take Mr Dee along to find a bed for the night? I'm sure there will be room in one of the nearby inns."

Samrarn, who was the driver of the hospital landrover, responded with a big smile. He was a friendly and hospitable man, and he didn't bother making enquiries at the inns. Instead he took Dee to his own home and welcomed him as a guest.

PART III

Chapter 13
New horizons

"There's no reason why I can't go and live in the temple!" Lamon insisted.

Plans were going ahead for Ploy's marriage to Jit, after which they would live in his village. Samart, now married to Keng, was still not happy to leave Lamon in the village without close relatives. But Lamon was just as determined not to live in a new area where people did not know her. At sixteen she felt she was old enough to decide for herself.

Finally they all went to visit their friend the monk. The Reverend Father listened patiently. "I've told you a number of times, son," he addressed Samart in fatherly tones, "that it will be best for Lamon herself and for all of you if she comes to live in the temple as a nun." The monk's voice was calm and firm.

"But surely this could make real problems for you," answered Samart questioningly. "I always understood that people with leprosy are not allowed into a Buddhist temple."

"That's what the rules imply," admitted the abbot,

"but I feel that we have to weigh up the situation and make our own decision."

"But the others living in the temple may object. They may even be afraid to have Lamon around, so if you insist on letting her in, they'll become angry." Samart knew that Lamon would be even more hurt if she were eventually turned out of the temple.

"That could be a problem in years to come, I suppose, but not in the foreseeable future." The monk sounded very confident. "You know, don't you, that Lamon comes to the temple quite often, and has a number of friends here. Some of the older women have expressed their concern for your sister and have told me they wouldn't object if she lived here."

"But what about the monks, and particularly the younger ones who will come during lent each year? They won't know her, so it could be a shock for them."

"You're a very pessimistic young man, Samart," said the abbot in an uncharacteristically sharp tone of voice. "Please trust me. I've promised to take care of Lamon and I will do so."

"All right," Samart said at last. "We'll try it. It would be a great help at the moment. I'll continue to visit her regularly and you must tell me immediately if there are problems."

The day came when these two young women left their old home for the last time. One attractive and lovely, leaving in great excitement and anticipating happiness as a wife and mother. The other going out in all her wretchedness and ever-worsening condition, facing a new life with a sickening uncertainty, not daring to think what the future might hold.

Ploy to enjoy her beautiful silk wedding dress and attractive hair-do; her pretty face to be admired by husband and guests at the wedding. Lamon to don the plain white cotton garments of a Buddhist nun, her already deplorable appearance to be exaggerated as her head would soon be shaved bald. No more than a creature to be rejected and despised as long as she might live, like leprosy sufferers the world over for generations. Hopeless, wretched, often living in deplorable conditions, lonely to a degree unimaginable to most normal people, leading all too often to extreme psychological and emotional imbalance. Total rejects from normal society.

In fact, compared to most of the world's leprosy sufferers Lamon was very favoured. To have a brother and sister who cared for her and had stood by her, and a Buddhist monk taking real risks on her behalf, was quite remarkable. But the truth remains that, had she left her village and the sheltered environment where everyone knew her, she would have met total rejection from the population at large.

"New medicine to cure leprosy! I can't believe it," exclaimed Samart to an acquaintance who was explaining to him about all the modern drugs beginning to trickle into the country in the late 1950's. "We've already tried so many remedies. Nothing will cure leprosy."

In spite of his disbelief, this conversation lingered in Samart's mind. He was well aware that new medicine shops were opening in town and that they stocked different medicine from the old herbalist shops. He decided to call and make enquiries.

"Yes, yes!" said the salesman in the medicine shop with great enthusiasm, when he heard Samart describing his sister's symptoms. "This is the 'woman's disease', isn't it? It can now be cured by giving an injection every day for three weeks," he asserted firmly.

"Three weeks!" Samart gasped as he thought of Lamon's ugly face with its thickened and wrinkled skin, and her ulcerated feet. *How can she get better in three weeks? A ridiculous suggestion!* "What do you mean by calling it the `woman's disease'?" he asked aloud. Other people had told him this, but his common sense had always denied it.

"Well, the symptoms you described sound like the advanced stage of one of the venereal diseases," replied the medicine man. "These injections are an excellent cure for syphilis."

"My sister does not have syphilis," shouted Samart, swearing angrily. "My parents were decent people, and my sister wasn't born with this disease. The first symptoms only appeared when she was five or six years old."

The shopkeeper realized he'd offended Samart and became very polite. "I agree, it doesn't sound possible for your sister to have VD," he said as he started to count out 21 small bottles of penicillin. "Actually this is very good medicine for many kinds of disease and infection. I'm sure it will do her good." He had no medical knowledge, no training in pharmacy, but he was a good businessman. "Can anyone in your village give injections?" he enquired.

"Yes, that's no problem. How much will all these bottles cost?"

Knowing that Samart was desperate to get the best quality treatment, the salesman quoted a high price, explaining that this medicine was imported from the west and was very expensive.

"Well, I suppose it won't do her any harm," said Samart naively. "I'll take it."

Lamon did not get any reaction to the penicillin, nor, quite remarkably, did she get an abcess in her buttocks from all those injections.

When Samart went to visit his sister a month later he wasn't surprised to find no real signs of improvement. Her feet ulcers had improved a little, but now, a week after the injections were finished, the infection was beginning to appear again. The ulcers were still as deep as they had been previously.

So, if this modern medicine was no good for Lamon, why did Samart continue to hear the rumours?

"There is definitely a new drug to cure leprosy," a friend insisted. "I know a man who is receiving the medicine. It's a white tablet, and he has to take one pill alternate days. He's been told he'll have to take it for years, but his condition will gradually improve. In fact there's already some improvement."

"Well then, where do I find this medicine?" asked Samart in desperation. This one vital fact his informer had apparently overlooked.

These precise details about the medicine would not leave Samart's mind. Once again he began to consider all the various people who dispensed medicine. There were quacks of every description, herbalists whose remedies Lamon had tried over and over again, and a variety of witch doctors using every imaginable incantation. *Who else will have the know-how to dispense modern medicine?* he asked himself over and over again.

"Why didn't I think of this place before?" Samart suddenly exclaimed out loud one day as he walked along the main street in Lopburi town. He was standing outside a government health centre! These places were comparatively new, and up-country clinics like this one didn't have a very good reputation. However, he had heard that such places did have modern medicine from abroad!

Once again he related Lamon's symptoms and condition to the doctor, who listened patiently to it all. As Samart's story unfolded a knowing look came over the doctor's face. "You mean the 'angel's-droppings-disease' don't you?" he questioned, giving this disease what he felt to be its most appropriate name. "Yes, there is now a curative medicine for leprosy, but it's still very new and I'm not allowed to dispense it here."

He told Samart that this treatment was only available at a few government clinics and hospitals. "However," he continued quickly before Samart's hope were dashed again, "go and see the foreigners."

"The foreigners!" echoed Samart in disbelief. "Where do they live? How can I find them? Do they have the medicine?"

"Yes, they have the medicine," the doctor assured him, "they have a clinic at the top of the hill at Tha Pho. I think they have it on a Tuesday."

"If these people are foreigners I suppose they speak English," Samart said. "How do I communicate with them?"

"No problem," answered the doctor. "They've learned to speak Thai. I believe they speak our language quite well, good enough to be understood. They are all women. I've heard that they are very diligent in their work, they seem to know all about this disease. They have many patients who are badly disfigured, men and women we Thai people hate and despise because we're afraid of this disease. But these foreign women don't despise them, nor are they afraid of leprosy."

Chapter 14
Samart the guinea pig

"Yes, I understand that this is the disease of leprosy and that your sister is very sick. But she must come here and be examined before I can give you any treatment for her."

"But I think you don't realize how bad she is," Samart said desperately. "The village where she lives is about thirty kilometres away. No vehicle can get into the village. I should have to carry her out, walking along the narrow dykes between the rice paddies."

"But won't some of your relatives help you to carry her out of the village?" asked the nurse at the Overseas Missionary Fellowship[1] leprosy clinic on the outskirts of Lopburi town. It was a Tuesday morning towards the end of 1959.

"We're a family of orphans, we haven't got any close relatives," Samart explained. "No one in the village cares whether my sister gets treatment or not. Even when I get her to the river, I should have to hire a boat

---

[1] See Appendix I for information on OMF.

to reach the main road. When the boat owners see her condition they'll ask an impossible price. Finally, if I ever do get her to the main road, she'd never be allowed on to a public bus."

...No one cares whether she gets treatment or not ..., the boat owner will ask an impossible price..., she'll never be allowed on to a public bus ... Nurse Eileen stood stunned in the midst of the busy clinic, these sentences ringing in her ears and stinging her heart. Indifference! It not only kept neighbours from giving help, but also caused people to exploit cripples and other handicapped people.

As tears threatened to well up in her eyes she looked into the face of the young man in his soldier's uniform.

A man! A soldier! she thought. *A young man too. Why is he here? Why does he alone seem to care so much for his sister? Why is his heart not hardened to apathy and indifference like most others?* A young soldier should be hardened by the normal processes of growing up. But he wasn't hard! He was concerned and anxious. He wasn't even ashamed that his own eyes were blinded with tears as he waited for the nurse to soften and give in to his request.

Eileen glanced around the small shelter-like structure that served as the leprosy clinic or *sala*, realizing Samart needed detailed explanation about leprosy and modern treatment. *How am I going to cope with him as well as all these other patients who've already been waiting for such a long time?* she wondered.

As well as the regular patients waiting for routine leprosy treatment, there were new people to be examined and diagnosed. All were suffering from various skin ailments; most did not have leprosy. They all needed time given to them, either for reassurance that they did not have leprosy, or for encouragement and assurance that leprosy can be brought under control with modern medicine.

In another corner of the clinic a second missionary nurse was persevering with a queue of patients waiting to have dressings done on the ulcers of their hands and feet.

The sun was getting high in the sky and its roasting rays beat down on the galvanized tin roof of the *sala*. *The temperature must be approaching a hundred,* Eileen thought as she suddenly realized how hot and sticky it was. *The humidity's atrocious today, I wish it would rain.*

"Nurse, my train leaves in about twenty minutes," a patient interrupted her thoughts. "I don't have enough money to get a pedicab to the railway station so I'll have to walk. Please could I have my medicine right away."

Eileen began to panic as she realized several patients needed to catch that train.

Samart stepped back. "Please let these patients go first," he said politely. "I can wait."

Eileen felt rebuked. *I'm a Christian missionary,* she told herself. *Why do I let circumstances get the better of me?* She prayed quickly for help, and knew what to do.

"Thank you," she said to Samart as she sat down at her table. "It will only take a few minutes to check these patients and give them their medicines, then we can discuss what to do about your sister."

The half-dozen people who wanted to catch the train left after receiving their tablets and a word of encouragement.

"Sit down and tell me about your sister." Eileen motioned Samart towards a seat beside her table. She was feeling relaxed now as she prepared to listen.

"Lamon was still very small when Mother noticed the pale patch on her arm," Samart began. "I'm ten years older, so I too used to watch the harmless-looking mark. Lamon never complained about it, it wasn't irritable or sore, but it gradually grew larger."

"Has your sister ever had treatment anywhere else?"

This question gave Samart opportunity to enlarge on the variety of treatments tried, including the time when the monk used the searing medicine to burn out the lesion. He also gave a vivid account of their visit to the medicine man, and the expensive herbs to which his younger brother had objected so violently.

By now Samart wasn't only speaking to the nurse. His dramatic story, told with a great deal of flourish and expression, had attracted the attention of all the waiting patients in the clinic. They were well entertained.

He left nothing out, emphasizing Lamon's gradually worsening condition: clawed hands, dropped foot, chronic ulcers, septic nodules continually coming and going all over her body, the changing appearance of her skin, face and ears.

"More recently I went into one of these modern chemist shops," he said in a sceptical tone of voice. "The shop owner made me very angry when he told me my sister has syphilis!" A sympathetic murmur came from the listeners, some of whom had had the same accusation hurled at them. "That man sold me 21 bottles of penicillin which were injected into my sister over a three-week period. It didn't do her any good at all," he told them indignantly.

"Did your sister have any adverse reaction to the penicillin?" Eileen asked, at last managing to stem the flow of information. "It's very dangerous medicine, you know."

"Oh!" he exclaimed. "I didn't realize. The man in the shop said it wouldn't do her any harm."

"I realize now that your sister does have a very severe form of leprosy, but I'm sorry I cannot allow her to have this medicine until I have examined her myself." Eileen spoke with authority.

"The thing that causes leprosy is a germ, a particularly strong germ," she continued to explain. "For someone like your sister who has had leprosy for so long, the germs will have multiplied to countless millions. Therefore the medicine has to be extremely potent in order to kill the germs. Many patients have severe side effects and become very ill with acute symptoms. Their bodies are reacting to a battle between the medicine and the germs. They need much encouragement to continue with the treatment. In the end the medicine will win the battle, but some patients fear they are going to die in the process, so they become unwilling to continue the treatment."

Samart, listening with interest, said nothing.

"If I give you the tablets and your sister takes them and becomes extremely ill, what will she do? You've already told me that she lives in a village where most people don't care much about her. You've explained how difficult it would be to bring her here. You yourself are a soldier, and presumably don't live in that remote village so you wouldn't be there to help her. Consequently she would probably stop taking the tablets, and that could make for greater difficulties in treating her later on. My orders from the doctor are that patients must be seen before they begin treatment. I must see her to establish a relationship of confidence and so ensure that she will be able to continue treatment once she starts."

Samart looked at her with dismay. He could understand what she was saying, but he couldn't believe that the medicine would be withheld for these reasons. He swore, and mumbled something that Eileen didn't understand.

Some of the patients nearby laughed. "She won't give in," someone called out. "These foreigners are not like us Thai people. If the doctor who is her boss says she mustn't give treatment until she's examined the patient, then she'll obey the doctor. These people really do obey the rules."

Samart sighed; he knew he had met his match for stubbornness.

"Another point is that I have to make a chart for all patients," continued Eileen. "It has to have a diagram of what your sister looks like before the treatment begins, so that we can compare it with her condition and appearance after several months of the medicine. I have to send this information to the government of your country every three months. The government along with the World Health Organization would like to stamp out this disease, so it's important that I send in correct information."

"Oh!" said Samart with fresh interest. He was impressed that the government was involved with treating this disease. Eileen sensed that she had scored a point, and went on to offer some practical help. "My colleague and I could go out to your sister's village to examine her there," she suggested. "We could explain directly to Lamon and the people she lives with all about this disease and the cause of it. Then we could start the treatment, and discuss what should be done if her condition worsens before it begins to improve."

Samart looked at Eileen with her fair hair, pale skin and slight build. "You'd have to walk for miles," he said, "on rough paths and across dry paddy fields where there's no shade from the sun. You might collapse before you're halfway there."

"I've been to visit patients in remote areas before," Eileen told him. "I agree that it isn't easy, but my friend and I have never collapsed."

"I shall have to think about it," said Samart doubtfully. "It's unheard of to take white women into our village. I'll have to discuss it with my friends and the abbot at the temple. You couldn't possibly go and come back on the same day, but I don't know where you could stay overnight.

"I do understand now that it's important for you to see my sister before she starts this treatment. I'm very impressed with your clinic and the thoroughness of your work, and I'll come back when I've discussed things with my friends. We'll either find a way to bring Lamon into the clinic or arrange for you to visit her."

"All right," said Eileen. "Come back soon, because I'm sure your sister needs the treatment very badly. Before you go, I'd like to examine you just to make sure that you haven't got any early signs of the disease, seeing that you've lived with Lamon for so long."

Samart looked amazed. "Examine me?" he questioned unbelievingly.

Eileen smiled. The other patients were greatly amused at his reaction, and several tried to explain to him that this was normal procedure.

"In order to find new patients and start them on treatment early," Eileen told Samart, "it's necessary to examine all the close relatives of patients."

Off came Samart's shirt at once when he understood - he was happy to be assured he was free from leprosy. And immediately the nurse caught sight of two very suspicious white patches on his back! He had no idea of their existence until Eileen told him about them.

"No, they are not irritable," he assured her. "I've never noticed any kind of abnormal sensation in that area."

Next Eileen asked him to take off his big boots. "Do you have normal sensation of pain in your feet if you stand on anything sharp?"

"Yes, so far as I know," he said a little hesitantly.

"Do you react normally if you pick up something that is too hot?"

"Oh yes," he answered confidently. After careful examination Eileen was satisfied that there was no numbness in his hands or feet.

Leprosy in its very early stages can be difficult to diagnose accurately. Pale patches on the skin are certainly among the first signs of the disease, but some types of vitamin deficiency and some kinds of tinea or other fungus infections also cause very similar skin lesions. Eileen looked carefully at the marks on Samart's back, taking him outside into the bright sunlight for a thorough examination. *This could well be leprosy*, she thought. *But perhaps it would be better not to tell him definitely.*

"In view of your close relationship with Lamon over many years," she summed up, "I'd like you to start a course of treatment yourself. This will destroy any leprosy germs in your body, and prevent the disease spreading."

Samart was grateful beyond words, and took the medicine without question - leprosy control tablets, vitamin pills and anti-anaemia tablets.

"Here's a supply of medicine for one month," Eileen told him. "Please come back to the clinic in four weeks' time." She pointed out that she had written the date on the medicine envelope for him.

As Samart walked away from the clinic that morning, he knew he would be back. He had a sense of relief and a confidence he had never known before. If Lamon could get help from anywhere, it was here. Even though he didn't know how he would get Lamon to the clinic, he was determined to find a way in due course.

Samart had been taking the treatment for four months. Now he was at the clinic again for another supply of medicine. Last time the nurse had told him that the white patches were fading. He had been faithful in taking the tablets, and his friends said they could see nothing abnormal on his back.

"Your friends are quite right," Eileen assured Samart. "The marks on your back have completely disappeared. But, as I've told you before, you should continue to take the treatment for a longer period."

"I don't mind at all," Samart told her. "It's cheap, easy to take, and I actually feel better and more energetic since taking this medicine. I presume it's the vitamins and iron tablets that make me feel so well." He grinned, and Eileen agreed.

However, there was another reason why he wanted to go on with the treatment. A new idea had begun to simmer in his mind. It might be dangerous, but he thought he would eventually try it out.

So far he had not told Lamon about these foreign nurses and the new treatment for leprosy. Each time he saw her he had intended to, but each time he found he couldn't let her know that he himself was suspected of having the disease. And he didn't have the heart to tell her that the nurse would not treat her until she had been examined. So far he had not worked out how to get her to the clinic. It seemed better to keep quiet for the time being.

And then this foolhardy idea started to grow in his

mind. He remembered all that the nurse had told him about the potency of the leprosy control tablets. He knew that it would be a risk. But the more he thought about his idea, the more he believed it was worth it. He decided to take the medicine himself for six months. After that, if he still had no adverse reaction to the treatment, his experiment would go ahead.

Chapter 15
Problems and plans

Samart was still very much in love with Keng. Their marriage seemed satisfactory and they were happy together. However, they were not without problems. Samart's spartan upbringing and the load of responsibility he had carried for his sisters made him seem older than his years. In her heart of hearts, Keng must have appreciated the fact that her husband did not drink, gamble or go off with other women. However, she grumbled that he was too melancholic, not interested in having fun. Both at home and at work he had the reputation of being a straight-laced miser! From poverty he had come into comparative affluence as a soldier. But old habits die hard, and Samart was slow to adjust to spending his money on anything but dire necessities.

Much of his money, in fact, went to support Buddhist temples, with a continuing cry to the spirit of Buddha to show mercy to his sister. He still hoped that his efforts to make merit might prove fruitful.

Every time he went to visit Lamon he took as much food as he could carry. Usually he chose dried and salted food - meat, fish, vegetables and candied fruits - so that Lamon would have some extras when temple rations were short. He also took food for the other monks and nuns in the temple.

Samart knew that their good friend the abbot, who had shown such love and kindness, was very much an exception. Probably not one other person in the temple shared the same sympathy, in fact they only tolerated Lamon because the head of the temple said she had to stay. So the food and gifts he took for them was by way of reward for their tolerance, and with the hope that they would treat her reasonably well.

In the early days of their marriage Samart had always told Keng when he planned to visit Lamon, and that he took gifts of money and food.

"Why are you going again?" asked Keng in an irritated tone one day when Samart told her he intended to visit Lamon. "It's only a couple of weeks since you last went to the temple. We'll never have any money if you go so often."

"Yes, it does take a lot of money," Samart agreed, quietly but firmly. "But you are a Buddhist too so you must believe that if I can make a lot of merit on behalf of my sister, she may get better, or at least come back in a better condition in her next existence."

There was no answer to that, so Keng remained silent. But her anger mounted.

"I warned your father before we were married what it would be like," Samart continued. "He should have told you what my intentions towards my sister were. Obviously he didn't get the point across."

"Don't speak about my father like that," Keng snapped. She turned away in a very bad mood, her heart full of resentment.

Samart left the house in silence, his mind in conflict.

Where does my loyalty lie? he wondered as he walked towards the bus stop. *I love my wife, I hate to argue with her. But I also love my sister and want to help her.* He had plenty of time to wrestle with his mental turmoil as he sat on the bus for the six kilometre ride along the bumpy road to Tha Khlong, and then got a boat that would land him within seeing distance of the village.

That day he decided he must continue visiting and supporting his sister - but in secret. He would never again tell Keng when he was going to see Lamon. From now on her name was taboo.

As Samart walked through the attractive grounds of the temple he saw some of the monks busy with odd jobs to keep the place tidy.

"Hello," he said cheerfully as he passed close by two of them, who had discarded their saffron robes and wore only a wrap-around pinafore type of undergarment.

"Hello," they replied. "When are you going to take your sister away?" one of them asked in an aggrieved tone.

"Not yet," said Samart, trying not to get ruffled. He walked on with an apparent air of indifference, but his heart was stinging. As he approached the building where Lamon spent most of her time, he wondered what sort of mood she would be in today.

Lamon was very depressed. She couldn't hide her feelings from her brother and her tears flowed freely. She knew it was no good asking Samart to take her away - there was nowhere to go. But she longed to be nearer so that he could visit more frequently. Samart knew all this. He also knew that if he talked too much about his own happiness, it would make her even more depressed. So he often found conversation difficult.

Samart could never forget the first day he had arrived at the temple as a proud father. Keng had given birth to a baby daughter, and his delight and pleasure knew no bounds. But as he related details of the birth, Lamon was overwhelmed by the sudden realization that she might never see this baby, her own niece, never know the joy of cuddling her, or playing with her as she grew up.

"Why do you come and tell me about this?" she asked him. "If I can't see your baby and play with her, I don't want to know about her."

Samart was shocked into silence. He had thought she would be as pleased as he was.

"I'm almost seventeen now," she reminded him. "I have normal feelings about the opposite sex. I'd like to get married and have babies. But what hope have I?

"None!" she answered her own question in the same breath.

"Keep your baby and don't come telling me about it," she screamed at him. "I suppose you and Keng will have several children, and soon Ploy will start having babies. You can all have families but I shall never have a baby." Her sentences were laced with swear words and cursing.

Samart was speechless. He had never seen her like this before.

"I want a husband to love me too, but it's impossible. I look worse than an animal. No men ever come near me, I'm only hated and despised. Why did you let me live? You could have taken me to the forest over the hill when I was still small. I should have lost my way and starved to death. It would all have been over now, and I should never have known this agony."

"Dear little sister," he said to her, putting his arm

around her shaking body as she sobbed uncontrollably. "My dear sister," he repeated again and again. "I love you, I will care for you, I'll do all I can to get you out of here eventually."

After Samart had left and Lamon recovered somewhat, her heart was filled with anguish. *What came over me? Will he really come back? Does he really still care for me? He told me that he would come again, I heard him say so,* she told herself. *But he may be so offended and hurt that he'll change his mind.* Such thoughts were a nightmare to her until the moment she saw him walking along the path towards the temple a few weeks later.

Ironically, when he came the next time, he was sad and depressed himself. His darling daughter had become very sick and died during the first few weeks of her life. Lamon was heartbroken, the news adding to the remorse she had felt since his previous visit.

Their relationship was restored instantly as her sympathy was lavished on him. They cried together and then were able to communicate in a way that had not been possible for several months. His disappointment and heartache had opened a door that enabled her to minister to him in a small way. It did wonders for her.

But this was another day. Again Samart was the bearer of what he felt to be thrilling news. *This time,* he thought, *she must surely be as excited as I am.*

It was late morning. The sun was already high and he had no shade for his six kilometre hike across the rice paddies. But he was so full of his plans that he didn't notice the tiring heat. He was almost running. "Little sister, Little sister," he began, "something wonderful has happened! I've found some medicine that can kill the germs that cause your disease!"

She looked at him with scepticism written all over her face. "We've tried so many kinds of medicine," she replied laconically. "I can't be bothered to take any more."

Her indifferent attitude took the wind out of his sails, and he hesitated for a few seconds, wondering how to continue. He recovered quickly, however, as he suddenly remembered that she knew nothing of his wanderings in search of this medicine for so many months, nor his own recent experiences.

He knew he had to tell her the whole truth in order to prove the power of the treatment. So he poured out the story: the government doctor's recommendation of the foreigners, the *sala* clinic up the hill on the outskirts of Lopburi city, the western nurse who could speak Thai and her attention to detail. Carried away with enthusiasm, he was telling her all this at great length when he suddenly realized that she still wasn't responding. She actually looked quite bored!

But Samart was a determined young man! He concluded that this must be one of her particularly bad days, and went on to tell her about the pale patches on his back.

"I couldn't see them for myself," he said, "but I understand that they were like the marks you had on your arms when you were small."

At this the boredom left her. She was aghast. "Are you saying that you have this disease also?" she blurted out.

"I did have it," he corrected her in triumph, "but I am better, I'm healed. I have to take this treatment for a longer period to make sure all the germs are killed, but if this medicine is good for me, it will be good for you!

"Because you're so bad, I expect it will take a long

time for you to get better. But never mind," he continued, his enthusiasm mounting again, "I believe with all my heart that it will work in the end. I've now been to the clinic six times," Samart went on without giving her the chance to interrupt. "I'm getting to know some of the other patients, and they all tell me the same thing - they are much better than they were. There's no doubt that they have the same disease as you, I've looked at their hands and feet. Some are even worse, much worse than you. One man has no fingers at all, others have got terrible ulcers on their feet, worse than yours have ever been, and yet they all insist that they are much improved."

Lamon was listening with greater interest now, but she didn't comment.

"Little sister, do you believe me? Will you try this medicine and see if it works for you? I've brought some of the tablets for you to begin today." This was the secret plan that had been taking shape in Samart's mind for the past three months. He was an intelligent young man. He had observed that the nurse started him off on a low dose of the leprosy medicine, and gradually increased it each time he went to the clinic. Now she had told him that he was on full dose. So he worked out how he could share his own tablets with Lamon, giving her the same kind of increasing regime as he had taken himself. He knew it meant that he would not be receiving the full amount, but he hoped that by the time his sister had taken the tablets for six months she would have improved slightly.

And then he would tell the nurse what he had done. If he could report that Lamon had had no adverse reaction to this drug, then surely Nurse Eileen would be willing for Lamon to continue whether she saw the patient or not! If she did still insist on seeing her, then

Lamon might feel better and be willing to make the effort to travel to the clinic.

Samart's enthusiasm was beginning to be infectious. Lamon could see he had great faith in the tablets, and also in the foreign nurses. So, even though she was a little suspicious of anything from outside Thailand, she told him that she would take the tablets and see if they had any effect on her. She had been disillusioned so many times that her hopes didn't soar too high.

"This medicine is very strong," Samart told her. "The nurse says it's potentially dangerous and could make you quite ill."

"Well, I don't want to become seriously ill," Lamon said doubtfully. "People here may not be keen to care for me."

"It's not had any adverse effect on me," Samart quickly assured her. "I believe you'll be all right, in fact I'm sure this medicine is going to do wonders for you. In a few weeks you'll feel much better, even though it will take longer for you to look better. As soon as you begin to feel better we must make the effort to get you to the clinic, so that you can meet the nurses and see the other patients."

Samart went away that day with great joy in his heart. He was convinced that his experiment was going to work.

Chapter 16
Samart on the brink

"**I** would like to buy a Bible," said a stern, somewhat irritated voice at Lopburi leprosy clinic one morning. "I appreciate all you're doing for my sister, and we're very impressed with the results of the treatment. But there's one thing that makes me angry when I come to the clinic."

The nurse was rather taken aback at this outburst, but she remained composed. "I'm sorry to hear that," she replied. "Perhaps if you explain what makes you angry, I could help put things right."

"I doubt it!" came Samart's blunt reply. "It's this matter of teaching your Christian religion. We Thai people are perfectly satisfied with our Buddhist religion, and yet as we sit here waiting to receive our medicine you virtually force us to listen to preaching about Jesus Christ."

"Yes, it must seem like that to some Thai people," the nurse agreed, wondering what was the best way to tackle Samart in his present mood. "But others are very interested, and ask intelligent questions about Jesus. A few have come to believe that the Christian Bible is the truth and are now trusting in the living God."

"I know that only too well! It's these Thai people who are believing that are such a nuisance! They know I'm a religious person, so they are for ever trying to persuade me that Christianity is better than Buddhism. I've tried to argue with them but they have learned the Bible well and know all the answers. That's why I want to buy a Bible. If I read it and study it for myself, I can compare it with Buddhist teaching. Then I shall know how to answer when you are telling me about Jesus."

This was not the first time that the clinic had seen a confrontation with Samart. But now he was actually going to buy a Bible! The nurse, and other Christians hearing the conversation, could scarcely conceal their excitement. This forthright, determined character would surely read the Bible if he bought it. And then, whatever his motive for reading it, God could overrule and change him as he read.

Months had now become years since Samart started to attend Lopburi clinic. He had eventually told the nurse about sharing his own treatment with Lamon. Eileen had been rather cross and very anxious at the time, but she realized this bending of the rules was one more thing that, as a foreigner, she had to accept about Thai people and their customs.

Samart could not be persuaded that he had done wrong. "What could the consequences have been anyway?" he argued. "I used my common sense, knowing the risk involved, but willing to accept the results if the experiment had gone wrong. When I explained the whole story to Lamon and she understood the potential dangers of this medicine, she welcomed the opportunity to try it out."

Eileen listened helplessly as he continued:

"My sister had often prayed for release from her

condition, you know. She truly did not wish to live if there was to be no improvement. Perhaps if this medicine had not worked for her, it would have killed her. Whatever had happened she felt she couldn't have been any worse off."

But the experiment had not gone wrong. The vitamins and iron tablets had worked rapidly. Within weeks Lamon was feeling like a new person and able to help the others with temple chores. The potent leprosy control tablets had had no adverse effects on her. Outward results came slowly, but at last one day someone told Lamon that her skin was looking better. The shrivelled appearance of her face was gradually giving way to a more normal complexion.

The nineteen year old's personality began to blossom quite remarkably. "Please bring a mirror for me," she requested her brother one day, after years of never wanting to see her own reflection. "I'd like to watch this miraculous process taking place in my body."

Lamon would probably never have been persuaded to make the journey to Lopburi clinic if she had not had some treatment first. As it was, she found the first journey in October 1960 distressing and exhausting, and was almost a physical wreck on arrival. But the effort was worthwhile. She saw other patients as bad as, and even worse than herself, just as Samart had told her. She met the foreign nurses, and also experienced something of the caring Christian fellowship.

"We really would like to visit Lamon at home," nurse Eileen told Samart as she prepared the packets of medicine for him to take. She had said this before, but always he had turned down the offer. So it was a pleasant surprise when he responded positively.

"You are very welcome. My sister and I have discussed the possibility and decided that it's a good idea. The abbot of the temple where my sister now lives is in favour of such a visit.

"When would you like to go?" he asked. "If possible, we need to go on my day off."

Eileen agreed. A date was set and arrangements were made.

This was the first of several visits to Lamon in the temple. The nurses were always pleased to go and Lamon obviously appreciated their visits. She and others in the temple enjoyed the diversion of the foreign women coming with all kinds of interesting chatter. They also seemed to like listening to the stories that the nurses told and the pictures they showed - tales about the creation of the world, and all kinds of amazing episodes from the life of their religious leader, Jesus. Buddhist history also had stories of miraculous happenings in the days when the Buddha was living and doing his good works. The difference was that these nurses seemed to believe quite firmly that the incidents in the Christian Bible were true.

"Amazing," concluded the nuns and monks in the temple. "We like to listen to our Buddhist miracle stories, but no adults believe that they are true."

The visits were a great boost to Lamon's morale. Every time they went she was full of thanks to them and sang their praises.

"We are working in Thailand and coming to visit you because God has urged us to do so," Eileen persistently explained to Lamon. "We're pleased to know that you appreciate us but it's important for you to show your gratitude to the Living God rather than praising us personally." Eileen and her colleague found it very embarrassing to receive such excessive commendation. "It's only as God has given intelligence and opportunity for research, that doctors have discovered this modern medicine," they explained.

This was a very strange concept for Lamon to grasp. These two young women were doing so much good in the world, and yet every time they were told how much merit they deserved, and in fact must be receiving, they denied it. All they would say was that Jesus inspired and helped them to do the work. They insisted that God must receive all the credit.

"Yes," Samart told Lamon, "I too keep thinking about all that merit making. That's one of the things that is persuading me to believe in Jesus. I've spent all this money on Buddhist merit making, but it's never done any good. You never got any better until you had this medicine. The nurses tell me that they pray for their patients every time they go to the clinics.

"It seems to me that the power of God is in this treatment. The nurse says that if He created us, then He can also heal our diseases."

Lamon was embarrassed and angry with him. "Well," she said, "you'll have to make your own decision about this Bible, but if ever you do believe in Jesus, please don't come here trying to fill my ears with that kind of talk. You must certainly never say things like that in the hearing of the monks and nuns in the temple.

"How can I ever face our faithful friend, the head monk," she asked her brother, "if you start to accept and go the Christian way? I shall be embarrassed to death, and our temple friends will think you are the most ungrateful person anywhere."

"I find it very offensive when you suggest that there's sin in my life."

Samart was in his aggressive mood again, and another argument was underway in the Lopburi clinic. "You obviously don't understand how much good I've done during my life. You know how badly deformed my sister is, and yet I've never hated or mistreated or neglected her. I try to help her all the time. I've spent thousands of baht to try and make merit and help her to be healed. I don't drink or smoke or gamble. How can you say that I'm a sinner?"

The Christians at Lopburi clinic had begun to look foward to Samart's visits. He always stayed to chat with them. Although their conversations were still argumentative, and Samart often got exasperated, they sensed that he had lost some of his confidence in Buddhism.

He hadn't even hinted to them the feelings he had expressed to Lamon. He still had so many questions that needed satisfactory answers, before he was likely to tell them that he was even considering becoming a Christian. However, it was obvious from his intelligent questions that he was reading his Bible.

Mr Ploog was a man quite badly deformed by leprosy - bad ulcers on his feet, some of his fingers gnarled and stiff, some gradually disappearing, and a face with all the typical leprosy deformities. But he was clean and tidy, wearing decent clothes, and his wavy hair brushed back to give him a smart appearance.

Samart didn't know Ploog very well, but he found him a likeable personality with an infectious smile. On the few occasions he had chatted with Ploog, he found he didn't want to argue but preferred to listen. Ploog's unassuming, calm attitude was a great help to Samart and seemed to bring peace to his heart. He guessed that Ploog was probably fifteen years his senior, and in spite of all his degrading deformities, Samart had a great respect for him.

So today, as Samart expressed his dilemma about being called a sinner, Ploog's confident testimony became one more link in the chain that was gradually leading Samart to faith in Jesus.

"You say you are a good man and have no sin; in that case you're just the opposite from me!" Ploog immediately reacted. "I know without doubt that before I became a Christian my life was full of sin. When I got this disease my family turned against me. They turned me out of the house and I had to live in a tumbledown shed in a corner of our compound. I became rebellious and depressed, so I turned to drink. I was almost always drunk, and I used to beat my wife and kids to get my own back on them."

This was a familiar story from leprosy sufferers, but now it was being told without resentment.

Ploog continued, "In order to make money to buy liquor, I used to keep fighting cocks. They're not difficult to raise and they bring a good price. I also made quite a bit of money by gambling at illegal cock fighting parties. So you see, there was no doubt that I was a sinner, and I knew it," he stressed. "My problem was that I didn't care. I was rebellious, and determined to remain bad.

"When I started to come to this clinic I could see there was a better way of life, but if my physical appearance couldn't be changed, I had no desire for my bad habits to be changed. If I couldn't be accepted into society again, then all I wanted was to continue hurting other people.

"So when you see me sitting here sober and harmless, you have to believe that some great power has taken control of my life.

"I've come to understand," continued Ploog with authority, "that it doesn't matter whether we're good or bad people, we all need this power in our lives, the changing power of Jesus Christ.

"Samart, you've told us yourself that you have all kinds of problems in your life, so even though you're a good and helpful person and often making merit, you're inadequate to cope with life. You need to know Jesus who is a real Person. He will help you and give you ideas and intelligence so you will know better how to sort out your problems."

There was a persuasive note in Ploog's voice now as he urged Samart to believe without further delay. "There's no need to wait until you have all the answers to your doubts." It was almost as though Ploog knew how Samart's mind was working.

"And regarding this matter of sin! If you can't accept that you're a sinner, you'd better read in your Bible about a man called Saul. He was an extremely good man in his own eyes and a faithful religious teacher. But when he eventually understood that Jesus was the Son of the living God, he could see that his goodness and religious knowledge and activity was a source of great pride, and that pride is a terrible sin in God's sight.

"Please excuse me for speaking so frankly," said Ploog with typical Thai courtesy, "but I think you are very much like Saul. Your life needs to be changed just as much as Saul's did, and just as much as mine did.

"Later on Saul's name was changed to Paul, and he became a great preacher. He was eventually imprisoned because of his faith in Jesus, but he never doubted. He often wrote letters to his Christian friends and these letters are also printed in the Christian Bible. I would advise you to read the letter Paul wrote to the Christians in Rome."

This was a long speech for Ploog. He was often very hesitant to speak out and draw attention to himself.

However, he had recently returned from Manorom Christian Hospital and all his friends knew that something had happened to him spiritually as well as physically during his stay in hospital. He had had plastic surgery on his face, [1] which made him less apprehensive when people looked at him. But his real confidence as he spoke out that morning, was because he now had absolute assurance that he was a member of God's worldwide family. He knew his sins were forgiven and that God loved him. He wished that Samart could get the same assurance.

---

[1] For further details see Appendix II

Chapter 17
Good news

Samart strode effortlessly across the hot, dusty fields towards the temple. His carefully-made plans kept turning over in his mind.

I'm sure they will stay around, he thought as a vision of shaven-headed, saffron-clad men flashed into his imagination. *We've had some good discussions recently, and they seem to enjoy hearing what I'm reading in the Christian Bible.*

His usually serious face portrayed how he was feeling today. The dark, penetrating eyes maintained their dogged determination, but his mouth, often taut with anxiety and aggressiveness, was relaxed. The smile on his lips caused his whole face to come alive. His forehead, frequently creased with a frown, was today smooth and without friction. Samart looked no more than his thirty years.

The timing's perfect, he thought, glancing at his watch as he entered the monastery compound and walked towards the *sala*, where the whole temple staff would be assembled for their eleven o'clock meal.

As Samart went up the steps into the building, all

heads turned to observe his arrival. He quickly noticed his sister and went towards her. She greeted him politely as he squatted beside her for a brief conversation.

"I have some great news today. I've made new arrangements for your future! The nurse says you can go into hospital! I'll give you the details later. I want everyone here to know, so when the monks have finished eating I hope to make an announcement before they all disperse."

He gave no opportunity for Lamon to respond, but rose and walked away from her, leaving her dazed and wondering if she had heard correctly.

Samart approached a group of lay workers who were sitting cross-legged on the floor, and sat down among them. He knew most of them well so he was soon chatting with them, while watching for the abbot to finish his meal.

At the appropriate moment he stood up and approached the dais where the monks were sitting. As he came face to face with his long-time faithful friend, Samart went down on his knees, bowed his head and raised his hands - palms together - in a respectful salute. Then he got up and went nearer to the abbot.

"I've made arrangements for Lamon to leave here, she's going into hospital," he said in a loud whisper. "Please may I have your permission to make an announcement while all the friends are present? I'd like to thank everyone for being willing for her to stay so long. And I have one or two other things to say also."

The elderly monk smiled and gave him a nod of consent, then stood up and called for silence. The murmur of voices quickly died away.

"Our friend Mr Samart would like to speak to us all," the abbot announced. "He has some important and interesting news. Please will everyone stay here and listen to Samart for a few minutes."

Samart coughed nervously. He had felt so confident as he walked across the fields rehearsing his speech. Now as he stood before this sea of faces his mind went momentarily blank. The silence was complete.

"You all know that I am Lamon's brother," he said, stating the obvious. This was not at all how he had intended to start.

"Yes," came back a loud response from the men in the audience. Everyone laughed, and Samart relaxed.

"Today I have some great news for you," he said, feeling more composed and able to think.

"First of all I want to thank you all very much indeed for allowing my sister to live here in this temple for so long. I hope you all understand that since Lamon started taking curative medicine for leprosy three years ago, her disease has become non-infectious. Even so, because of her appearance, I realize that it was difficult for most of you to have her around. We Thai people do not understand this disease, we're afraid of it, so we often dread and even hate the people who have it." He hesitated. There was silence.

"So I want you to know that I think you've been most courageous. You must have earned a great deal of merit for your patience and acts of kindness towards my sister ..." He went on like this, piling up even more lavish remarks, trying to impress them with his gratitude.

"Before I tell you what is going to happen to Lamon in future, I have something else to say about myself." He took a deep breath.

"Many of you know that ever since I found the leprosy clinic with the foreign nurses, I have been exposed to teaching about Jesus Christ. During these years I've been angry when the people at that medicine *sala* in Lopburi tried to influence me to believe in God - the so-called Creator God." He detailed how he tried to withstand the pressure, believing that Buddhism was the only religion for Thailand.

"Some of you know also that a while ago I bought a Christian Bible, in order to learn about Jesus' teaching and thereby be equipped to argue with the believers. We here have had some good discussions about it, haven't we, comparing Buddhism with Christianity.

"Today I feel that I must be honest with you, therefore, and tell you that after all my arguing with those Christians, and all my fighting against God, I've now come to believe that Jesus Christ is the Son of the Creator God. I've accepted what the Bible teaches. I have become a Christian."

A small murmuring broke the silence at this last statement. Samart glanced nervously at the abbot. The older man sat still with a knowing smile on his face. He was not surprised at what he was hearing.

As the abbot noticed Samart look at him, he realized that the young man feared he would be hurt or offended. "You are free to choose your own religion in this country, son," he said, just loudly enough for everyone to hear. "The Thai government does not forbid any religion. True religion draws us all together."

Samart sighed audibly. What a relief to know that his dearest friend did not condemn him! Finally then he dared to look over at Lamon. Her face was flushed and he presumed she was angry. She wasn't looking at him but was only interested in the reaction of the other nuns.

As the women heard the abbot's remarks, they all smiled and nodded at each other. Samart heard

Lamon's characteristic little giggle, as in spite of herself she visibly relaxed.

Ah, he thought, *if she sees the others don't condemn me, perhaps she too can accept my new faith.*

"Finally," he said aloud, "I want to tell you about Lamon's future." Silence quickly returned.

"I am soon going to take Lamon away from this temple. She won't be a burden to you any longer. She's going to be a patient at Manorom Christian Hospital and have operations to try and straighten her fingers and correct her dropped wrist." He asked her to hold up her hands to emphasize his point.

"These operations and treatment take a long time, so she will stay in hospital for many months. When the surgery is completed she'll be discharged from hospital, but I now have hopes that she'll be able to go and live elsewhere. She won't come back to this temple." This was as much a bombshell to Lamon as to the others.

Now the monks and nuns all began to comment and ask questions. Some were relieved that she wouldn't be there to bother them any longer. A few were interested in the possibility of surgery; they had watched her skin condition improve since she started taking the tablets, and now were pleased that her appearance could be improved even more. Others were relieved to have her go because they had always been afraid of catching leprosy from her.

Without exception, all were curious about Manorom Christian Hospital, wanting to know everything that Samart could tell them about it. They all seemed to have forgotten about the earlier part of his speech. No one commented about him becoming a Christian, showed hostility towards him, or suggested he was a traitor to his country or to Buddhism. There was no accusation of ungratefulness.

Samart was thrilled with everything about his new faith and was continually talking about it. He was getting used to sarcasm and cynicism. The hostility and rejection he had received from his wife and her family were indescribably painful for him, but they made no difference. He had been warned that being misunderstood was part of becoming a Christian. He was also having an extremely hard time in his army office because of his stand for right and honesty and his new fight against corruption. So nothing that anyone in the temple could have said against his faith in Jesus would have even rippled the surface for him.

And yet his characteristic Thai cunning and shrewdness had come to the fore as he had prepared his speech. He deliberately waited to announce his conversion until he had specific news about taking his sister to the hospital. He had planned it this way as a shield for her. He knew she was angry with him for "changing his religion", and that she feared and dreaded what the temple friends would say about him when he left.

Samart suspected, however, that deep down she was not so angry with him as it appeared. He had hopes that she would become a Christian in due course. But she had to maintain this attitude of disapproval before the others as a weapon of defence, in case they should turn against her because of his Christian faith.

As often as he heard something good about Manorom Hospital, Samart had passed the information on to her.

"I wish I could go there," she had said once, as he told her about Mr Ploog's surgery. That was enough for him. Immediately he had hurried to the clinic to ask the nurse if there was any hope.

"Every hope," Eileen said. "Of course she can go to the hospital."

Samart had one final piece of information to give his sister on this special day. He had not dared to tell her earlier.

"Keng has had another baby - we now have a son. I'm a father at last!"

He hesitated briefly to observe her reaction.

"This baby boy is strong and keeping well," he continued joyfully. "Now that you're so much better, and after your treatment in hospital, I'm sure you'll be able to see your nephew."

Now it only remained to tell her very precisely which day he was coming to take her to the hospital.

Lamon flung her arms around his neck as though she were a child again. "I can hardly wait!" she said.

PART IV

Chapter 18
Tawat at Manorom

"*The Christian* at Manorom is certainly different from any other hospital I've ever been to," reported Mr Dee to his family in Takhfa when he arrived home several days after the shooting incident.

They were keen to hear all about everything that had happened.

"Everything that can possibly be done for Tawat is being done," he assured them. "I was able to come home with an easy mind today, as I'm sure that Tawat is now out of danger. The doctors have warned me that the leg is very badly damaged and will take a long time to heal, but with care and attention Tawat should eventually be able to walk normally again."

Along with Mr Dee's favourable impression of the care and attention that Tawat was receiving, went his never-ending amazement about the cleanliness at Manorom Christian Hospital.

"The bed linen is clean, the floors are washed every day, the walls are swept frequently, and even the toilets are clean and don't smell," he told all his interested friends wherever he went. Nor did he forget the reception they had received when they arrived so late at night. The doctor's immediate appearance, the X-ray department, the path lab and operating theatre all functioning as though it was mid-morning, were a never-to-be forgotten feature of the place.

Bound to his bed in the ward, Tawat quickly became aware that many of the staff were different from all his previous associates. Not only the missionaries, but a number of the Thai staff also were Christians. He particularly enjoyed his doctor, the tall Australian who had done so much for him that first night. With his droll sense of humour that took Tawat's fancy, he quickly became the young man's hero.

For a long time Tawat's leg did not make good progress. Both the tibia and fibula bones were splintered, and he had to have a number of operations with reapplications of plaster casts each time. So Tawat stayed in hospital for months. He didn't mind at all. He often thought that even heaven couldn't be any better than this!

Once his general condition improved he was allowed to be up and about, first in a wheelchair and eventually on crutches. The general atmosphere was very relaxed. He was able to move around the hospital freely and get to know the young men of his own age who worked in the various departments, and the Thai nurse aides who paid so much attention to him, eager to answer his calls as often as he needed anything!

Tawat enjoyed sitting out in the shady grounds watching the outpatients come and go, sometimes chatting with pedicab drivers. At times too he enjoyed his own company, whether sitting outside or lying on his bed with the electric fan going on a hot, humid afternoon! An electric fan was a great novelty.

How long will they allow me to stay in this place? he asked himself one day after many weeks in the hospital. That morning his plaster had been removed, he had been to X-ray, and now he was confined to bed again for two days until a new plaster cast dried out. The doctor had told him that his leg was far from healed, and depression threatened to overcome him again.

I wonder why my leg takes so long to heal? What if it never gets really better? Supposing I become a cripple ... I'll lose my job and prospects for the future. I shall have to leave this place sometime, even if I'm not a hundred percent fit. Where shall I go? What shall I do?

Such thoughts brought back to his mind the poverty, despair and insecurity of his childhood. Panic gripped him. The vicious circle continued through his more recent experiences - the shot ringing out, the pain, the fear, the havoc within himself at that time, the nightmare journey through darkness and rain.

Why did this have to happen to me? he wondered. *Life has been so good recently.* He had thought he was enjoying life, and had become a man - drinking, gambling, doing all the things that men do. *But life like this is only possible when I can earn a wage and have plenty of money to spend.*

In his heart of hearts he knew that, even when he had appeared to be enjoying that kind of life, he had occasionally had forebodings that it could lead to disaster. Perhaps it had already done so.

Why was the shot fired anyway? he questioned. *It was meant for Mr Dee because he is rich, but if I become rich I may be the target another time.* The climax of this vicious circle brought dreadful uncertainty and conflict as he thought of his fiancée.

Tawat was seriously disturbed each time a vision of

this young woman drifted into his mind. He realized that he had been infatuated with her, but he was not really in love with her.

She often came to visit him during his stay in hospital, but as the weeks went by, he became less and less excited by her visits. It wasn't that any other girl had come into his life, but for the first time he was learning that there was far more to life than money and marriage.

But what can I do about it? I'm engaged to her and committed to her family. If I break off the engagement I shall have to leave the job. He faced the dilemma. *I shall lose face, I can't possibly stay on and work there if I don't marry her.* Because of the accident the wedding had been postponed, but no one imagined that it would not take place.

So a battle raged in his mind. Sometimes he felt he couldn't face a lifelong involvement with that family. Other times he told himself he was a fool to let this opportunity pass. *Once I'm back with them I'll soon revert to their ways and become my old self again.*

But what's happening to me? the questions went on in his mind. *I feel as though I don't want to be like my old self!* More and more he was coming to appreciate this Christian environment. His old way of life became very distasteful to him. Here cleanness prevailed - not just the cleanliness of the bed linen and floors and toilets, but something in the lives of his new friends that he could only describe as cleanness. It stood out in stark contrast to what he had always known as the norm: deceit, stealing, drinking, gambling, immorality, and the inevitable results: poverty, despair, distrust, revenge and hostility.

To his relief, as weeks became months, the vicious circle began to give way to a new chain of thoughts and considerations. He was alert, watching the lives of his new friends, both Thai and foreigners.

"If there's any appearance of cleanness or goodness or difference of any kind in my life," he was told repeatedly, "it's because Jesus Christ is a living Person. He has cleaned out the old and wretched things from my life." All his Christian friends told him that Jesus alone had been able to change their attitudes and bring right and decency into their lives.

As he listened to these stories he began to think back to his days as a Buddhist monk. The teaching about meditation and all the unhealthy introspection that comes with it. The claim that the only way to perfection and holiness is to suppress all one's emotions - anything attractive and beautiful is to be shunned, as it only distracts one's thinking and leads away from the truth. Warnings that even true love between the sexes, in fact close relationships of any kind, should be avoided - they can only bring disappointment and heartache, as all partnerships inevitably come to an end. And then all the theory about doing good and paying out money in order to make merit.

No wonder Tawat had been disillusioned and felt Buddha's standards impossible to attain. Now he was reading from the Christian Bible - about the creation of the world, for instance.

"The Creator God looked at everything He had made and was pleased," he read out loud. "That means that God actually took pleasure in and enjoyed the beautiful things of nature!"

On reading further he discovered that Jesus did not suppress His emotions. He went to parties and enjoyed Himself, He appreciated His relatives and friends and had close relationships with a number of people. He wept when those he loved died. Jesus had an astute and intelligent mind as well as a real sense of humour. Tawat told himself that all this was worth thinking about.

Jesus accepted both the good and bad of this world, but He was not naïve. He aimed to challenge people by His positive attitudes and strenuous activities for good as well as by His teaching.

These are the answers to life that I've searched for for years, Tawat suddenly realized one day as he read the Bible and other Christian books.

Then he began deliberately to find out about some of the Thai Christians in the hospital.

"I was a Buddhist monk for fifteen years," the business manager, Mr Arporn, told Tawat. "But I became disillusioned with the inconsistencies in Buddhist teaching. I deserted the priesthood after studying and taking many exams in Buddhism. I would soon have qualified to be a professional lecturer in our national religion."

If he is the business manager of a hospital he must be intelligent, thought Tawat as he listened to this story.

"I eventually decided that it was better to be a good Buddhist lay person than a bad monk," he told Tawat with a chuckle. "As you know, there are so many forbidding laws for monks, I found it totally impossible to keep them all. I was living a lie all the time. Later I went to study English language with some missionaries. While visiting their home I also read the Christian Bible, and found the truth in Jesus Christ. After a lot of consideration I renounced my national religion and became a Christian. It was a very hard thing to do, but it was the only way I could be honest with myself." This man especially was able to help Tawat sort himself out and think through the claims of Christianity.

The young man working in the path lab, Mr Samyong, had an exciting story to tell. He was a popular musician and singer.

"I used to be an actor in a Thai theatrical troupe," he told Tawat. "I lived a wretched life of immorality and drug addiction. Since I got to know Jesus and trusted in His power, my life has been completely changed. My old habits are gone, and the craving for drugs and liquor has miraculously disappeared. I believe that Jesus died in order to clean the sin out of my life. Now God has forgiven me. I'm like a different person."

A number of Thai friends were able to tell similar stories about themselves. And what about the foreigners, the so-called missionaries? Yes, all of them that he knew well enough to ask could tell remarkable tales of changes in their lives since they got to know about Jesus Christ and believed that He was a real Person, alive today.

Alive in these days! Tawat thought. *Strange book, this Bible! So much of it is good, but then I read stories about Jesus coming to life again!* He tried to analyze this theory in the light of his understanding of reincarnation, and his memories of lifeless bodies in their coffins. The practicalities of a literal resurrection were beyond his comprehension.

No, I simply cannot believe this, he concluded. *It must have been His ghost that Jesus' friends saw.*

Tawat read and argued with himself for many days. At last he decided to talk to his doctor friend. A man intelligent enough to study medicine would be able to give some reasonable explanation about Jesus returning from the dead. He was amazed and dumbfounded to hear that the doctor believed Jesus' reappearance and the other miraculous things mentioned in the Bible really happened.

"If you think that so much of the Bible is good, then why don't you test this Creator God?" challenged the doctor. "I am telling you that God is real. Why don't you talk to Him and ask Him to help you believe that Jesus Christ is really His Son and did return from the dead. And that He is still alive today?

"I know without doubt," the doctor continued, "that if you are honest with God, tell Him all your problems and doubts, and make sure you don't have a hard heart or a biased mind, then God will be able to answer you. He will make you just as sure as I am that the Bible is true."

This was not easy for Tawat. He knew that he did have a biased attitude. But he went on reading the Bible and observing his Christian friends, and by degrees he capitulated. He decided to take up the challenge and put God to the test.

One day the doctor, the nurses, and everyone knew that Tawat had given in to God. He was a new person.

Did he imagine that, if he became a Christian, all his problems would go away? If so, he was about to experience a great letdown.

What were these strange-looking marks on his skin? Some he could observe himself on arms and trunk, and the missionary staff told him about others on his back. After a thorough examination by the doctors and a skin smear test, Tawat was found to be suffering from a severe type of leprosy. It was still in its early stages, definitely curable. But undoubtedly leprosy.

Chapter 19
Is it really leprosy?

"**D**o you work here?" Tawat asked with surprise as a young foreign woman in a wheelchair approached him. He noticed that she was carrying a tray of equipment on her lap, and there was an air of belonging about her.

"Yes, I do," she answered cheerfully. "I work in the leprosy path lab."

Tawat had often seen her wheeling herself around the hospital compound, but because of her wheelchair he had assumed she was a patient. "Why are you always in a wheelchair?" he asked, curiosity getting the better of him.

"I became paralyzed when I had polio a few years ago. I was living in Inburi at the time."

"And how can you work if you don't walk?"

"Oh, there are lots of jobs that can be done with the hands. I used to be a nurse and so when this happened I was afraid I might not be able to work again. But when my condition improved I was able to study path lab technology. Eventually I was invited to come and work here in the leprosy department."

"I'm glad you mentioned the word leprosy," Tawat said. "The doctor has just told me today that I've got leprosy, but I don't understand what this disease is. Perhaps you could explain it to me."

Jean Anderson knew she faced a difficult task in telling Tawat about his disease. She felt she had to be honest with him, but she didn't want to frighten him unnecessarily.

"This is an infectious disease," she began. "The symptoms you have are the very earliest signs of leprosy. In these days of modern medicine there's every chance you will recover completely. The medicine is very strong, and it's been available in Thailand only for about ten years. So you are fortunate that you didn't get leprosy as a child."

As Jean chatted with Tawat she was beginning to prepare her equipment for taking a skin test from him. He watched her with interest.

"People who had leprosy before the germ-killing medicine came have had very difficult lives," she continued. "The infection spread uncontrollably throughout their bodies and caused them to become disabled."

Tawat went hot and cold. "But all I've got are a few blotches on my skin!" he protested. "Surely these can't be very serious?"

"Don't worry about it," Jean tried to assure him. "If you take the treatment and do what the doctor tells you, you will be all right. You'll get better. Now, please take off your shirt. I have to take what we call skin smears from several sites on your body where the marks are, and I need to have a good look at you first."

He readily complied.

"I have to make tiny nicks in your skin," she explained, "and then quickly scrape serum from under the superficial layer of skin. It may hurt a little but nothing to complain about."

With the number and type of lesions Jean could see on his trunk and arms, she knew that the germs were already well established all over him. She needed to take smears of serum from six widely-spread areas of his body.

Tawat winced slightly as she made her first quick jab, in his ear lobe.

As the procedure continued, Jean was feeling rather concerned for Tawat. She sensed that he still didn't understand what disease he really had. But if, as she suspected, the results of the test were positive, it would mean he was highly infectious. Then he would have to be moved from the general ward into the leprosy wing in order to protect other patients from infection.

Jean knew that at that stage Tawat would be in no doubt about what was wrong with him. He would see severely affected leprosy sufferers with his own eyes. *How will he react?* she wondered.

"Are you telling me that I have the same disease as these disfigured people?" Tawat asked the nurse in utter disbelief, when he found himself moved to the leprosy wing the following day.

"Yes," she answered. "These marks you have are typical leprosy lesions, and the results of the skin smears taken yesterday show there are many, many leprosy germs in your body."

Tawat was dumbfounded. He had had such faith in the staff of this hospital. "There must be some mistake," he argued.

The nurse was very sympathetic, realizing how desperate he must feel. She tried to explain, as Jean had done the previous day, that modern treatment is very effective and that the patches on his skin would most likely disappear quite quickly.

But Tawat simply could not accept that he had leprosy. He became angry and rebellious. For many days he sulked, depressed to a degree he had never known before. His good friend the doctor came to talk with him, trying to reason with him and explain about the progressive stages of leprosy.

"Please trust us, Tawat," the doctor pleaded. "You are actually very fortunate to be in this hospital when these skin lesions were discovered. Here we have trained staff to deal with this disease, and the necessary medicine to treat it immediately." The doctor was sympathetic, but spoke with authority.

"We had to move you out of the general ward because you're infectious at the moment. It would be dangerous for the other patients if we allowed you to stay there. But I can guarantee that, if you take the treatment, you will make a good recovery. Your leg's much better now, and it won't be too much longer before you're ready to leave the hospital."

Tawat heard what his doctor was saying, but he still could not accept the diagnosis. He was confused and filled with self-pity. However, he did not lose his new faith in Jesus. If anything, this experience strengthened his faith. He was not angry with God, only with the doctors and nurses, because he was so sure they were making a mistake. His main anxiety for himself was that he would get leprosy soon if he stayed in this leprosy-infected ward!

During these silent, unresponsive days, the only thing he could think of was to pray to God to make the marks go away, so that these people would realize they had made a mistake.

"Time for tablets," announced an attractive Thai

nurse aide as she walked into the ward carrying a tray with a variety of medicines. In spite of his bad mood Tawat did notice how pleasant she was.

"Here are some for you, Tawat," she said, handing him a container with three tablets. "One is a vitamin, another iron, and the tiny white one is the leprosy control tablet."

He didn't quite dare to refuse them, so he took them without a word. He had no choice but to swallow down the pills while the nurse stood and watched. The powerful drug was doing its work in Tawat's body.

Within weeks the leprosy lesions were fading. Tawat began to cheer up, and made good friends with a number of the leprosy patients. *They seem very nice normal folk*, he decided at last, *in spite of their deformities and ugliness*. Many of them were Christians, so as he came out of his shell he was able to enjoy fellowship with them and join in their Bible studies. He also noticed that his friends the hospital business manager Mr Arporn and path lab technician Mr Samyong often came to spend time with the leprosy Christians. The business manager sometimes stayed for hours, sitting close beside some of the most deformed patients, studying the Bible with them, even touching them as he helped them turn over the pages.

It can't be too infectious, concluded Tawat as he observed these frequent sessions and was convinced that Mr Arporn had no signs of leprosy.

The doctors and nurses were jubilant when his lesions subsided, convinced it was a result of the treatment. Tawat too was relieved, but he was still unconvinced that he had leprosy. *No point in arguing with them*, he thought smugly. *I believe that these discol-*

oured patches are fading as a result of prayer. What does it matter anyway, so long as they really do go away.

The first time Mr Dee and his daughter came to visit after Tawat's move to the leprosy wing, they were terribly shocked. Tawat showed them the patches on his body, told them what the doctor said it was, and then gave his own opinion of mistaken diagnosis. Mr Dee too found it hard to believe that these few harmless-looking lesions could possibly be leprosy. So to Tawat's face he agreed and sympathized with the young man.

However, he was not really convinced that Tawat was right. So he went to look for his doctor friend and to hear the explanation for himself. And he chose to believe the doctor.

The knowledge that Tawat had leprosy put Mr Dee in a dilemma. How could he allow his daughter to marry someone with this disease? Yes, the doctor assured him that Tawat would recover. *But he may get it again,* Mr Dee thought with genuine anxiety. *What a coincidence that it should show up in Tawat just at this time. Perhaps this will help to solve another uncertainty. I must think carefully.*

He had discerned for some time that Tawat's affection for his daughter had cooled, and that she was not missing Tawat as she had at first. So Mr Dee went home to consider how to deal with these matters without making anyone lose face.

He also knew that Tawat was now professing to be a Christian. At first he thought it would be a passing fancy, but now he could see there was a very real and apparently lasting change in Tawat. He certainly admired these foreign doctors and nurses and all that went on in their Christian hospital, but he couldn't see how Tawat could fit into the setup in Takhfa if he was so religious. He even sensed that Tawat knew this too.

Within a short period Mr Dee was back to visit Tawat again. "I called to see the doctor before I went home the other day," he told him.

Tawat felt startled.

"He said that you ought to continue the treatment for quite a long period. I hope you'll do so, to be on the safe side."

Hm! He believes the doctor then. He accepts that I have got leprosy, thought Tawat. He remained silent, wondering what the older man's reaction was going to be.

"The doctor was very good, he chatted with me for quite a while, explaining about this disease," Mr Dee continued. "I used to think leprosy was one of the venereal diseases, but he assured me that it isn't."

Tawat was feeling very tense.

"He said that your leg is almost healed now. You'll be able to leave the hospital before long. So I shall have to make arrangements for you to start work again."

Tawat sighed with relief. *So he isn't hostile, he doesn't condemn me for having leprosy, even if he does believe the doctor.*

Mr Dee continued to speak. "That is, if you really want to come back and work in Takhfa. Perhaps you think it's a dangerous, undesirable area and you may not wish to work with me any more." He hesitated, and looked straight at Tawat.

The young man remained silent, still uncertain what Mr Dee was implying.

"I have the impression that you rather enjoy being in hospital. Perhaps they will give you a job here, seeing you have so many friends and now appreciate the

Christian atmosphere so much." Mr Dee couldn't resist this guarded gibe as he felt somewhat out of patience with Tawat and his excessive religious tendency.

If Tawat recognized the remark as sarcasm he ignored it. This was a new idea! Such a thought had never crossed his mind, but now the seed was sown it was a very pleasant idea. He reacted with delighted surprise.

Mr Dee noted this with satisfaction. He was tempted to add a warning that he might soon become a puppet of the foreigners, but he managed to check himself, knowing that such a remark would surely indicate his true feelings. To him Buddhism and Thai nationalism went hand in hand. So he was conscious of a growing contempt for his fellow Thai who worked in a hospital run by foreigners. Particularly for those who had become Christians.

"I do like being here at Manorom," Tawat was saying. "The peaceful atmosphere is a great help to me. But I'm not afraid to go back to work in Takhfa," he said truthfully. Then he lied, "I never thought of going anywhere else."

The two were silent for a few moments.

Mr Dee was still sympathetic towards his employee, and remembered that the young man had worked hard and been very reliable. He wouldn't have given his consent to Tawat's marriage into the family if he hadn't thought him suitable.

But now he has leprosy, thought Mr Dee for the hundredth time. *Rook Khi Thut, the disease of angel's droppings. Why does he have this disease? Where did he get it from? Did his mother have it? Is that why she left her family?* Questions like these had plagued Mr Dee since he first heard the news.

Even if what the doctor told me is true, Mr Dee said

to himself, *that he will recover, that it will be safe for him to live with my daughter - how can I be 100% sure? And the doctor couldn't guarantee that his children will never get it. I like Tawat, but I simply can't allow him to come back or to marry Lek.*

Simultaneously, conflicting thoughts and questions were whirling around in Tawat's mind. *I'm definitely not scared to go back to Takhfa,* he thought. *But in truth I don't want to return. I know now that I don't want to get married yet. I'm not in love with Lek now, and I feel sure she doesn't care for me any longer either. And yet I do need some work. What shall I do if I don't go back there? No one has given any hint that I could work here. I have no training for work in a hospital.*

His thoughts next flitted to his new friend Wisut, whom he had met since coming into the leprosy ward. Wisut was a little older than Tawat, and his home was also in Saraburi. He had already suggested that he might be able to help Tawat find work in their home town.

Seeing that Mr Dee has been to talk to the doctor and he obviously believes I have leprosy, mused Tawat, *then he probably doesn't want me to go back to work with him or to marry Lek. I suppose that's why he's talking to me now. ... Yes! That's it! Mr Dee doesn't want me to marry Lek! I don't want to marry her. And I'm pretty sure she doesn't want to marry me.*

Having worked this out in his mind, Tawat broke the silence. "One big problem about going back to Takhfa," he began, "is that I don't think Lek is in love with me. She doesn't come to see me very often now, and when she does come we don't seem to know what to talk about. It isn't fun to be with her any longer."

"I agree, this is a problem," said Mr Dee solemnly. "I have actually questioned Lek about her feelings for you. She admits that she doesn't think about you like she used to do. Also, I notice that she's quite friendly with other young men at the moment. Though I can't blame her for that when you're not there!" he added with a chuckle.

"What about your feelings for Lek?" Mr Dee challenged Tawat directly.

"It's hard to say," he answered honestly. "I think if I were back in Takhfa and things were as they used to be, we should soon get to like each other again. But to be quite honest," he continued, "I've had a lot of time to think while I've been in hospital. I've decided I don't want to get married to anyone yet."

"Hm," murmured Mr Dee.

"One thing is sure," Tawat went on. "If I don't marry Lek, I can't go back to Takhfa. It would be too embarrassing for both of us."

"That's true," agreed her father. It was as though they were arranging a cold business deal. But it was working out as Dee had hoped. He hadn't had to forbid Tawat from going back to Takhfa. He had avoided confrontation on the leprosy issue. There were no hostile feelings between them.

"So do I understand you correctly then?" asked the employer. "You would prefer to go your own way and not return to my place?"

"That is my decision," asserted Tawat.

"Well, I enjoyed working with you, son," Mr Dee declared positively. "I liked having you around. You were dependable. I'm sorry you are not going to return."

Tawat blushed with embarrassment.

"Perhaps later on, when you feel like settling down, you'll come back and see me." Mr Dee felt he could risk saying this, even though he didn't really wish to see

Tawat again. He believed that this still somewhat naïve young man had got the point.

"By the way, all your bills are paid up to date," Mr Dee added. "The doctor says you will be leaving the hospital within a month. I'll come again in four weeks and pay anything else that's owing."

Tawat lifted his hands to his face in a courteous salute. "Thank you very much," he said.

Chapter 20
Surprises for Lamon

"This is Miss Lamon," said the missionary nurse as she showed the new patient into the pleasant four-bedded ward. "She's from Lopburi province."

"Oh!" exclaimed Mrs Boontom with pleasure. "That's good, I'm from Ban Mi district of Lopburi province. Which district are you from?"

"From Tha Wung," answered Lamon excitedly. "My home is in a village beside Samokhon mountain, on the border of Tha Wung and Ban Mi districts. We're close neighbours!" Her face beamed.

"Hurrah!" said Boontom as she clapped her hands and laughed. "Another one from the south!"

"From the south?" repeated Lamon, puzzled.

Boontom laughed again. "From one of the southern provinces of Central Thailand, I mean. Several of us come from down there, you'll soon meet them.

"This is Miss Yupin," continued Mrs Boontom, turning to a young woman lying in the next bed. "She's very unwell at the moment, but the doctor is hoping she'll get better without deformities."

Lamon took a look at Yupin and groaned. She could see at a glance that Yupin's body was covered with lumps and bumps just as her own had been a few years earlier. "I used to be like that," she said sympathetically. "I know you must be feeling very ill."

"Yupin has got a boy friend," said Boontom cheerfully. She turned her head to look out of the wide open window. "Isn't that true, Mr Win?" she asked a man sitting just outside in the corridor.

The young man lowered his eyes and put his head down.

"He's shy," she teased with a giggle. "Win comes from Khoksamrong district of Lopburi province," continued the vocal Mrs Boontom. "You'll get to know him well. He sits here most of the time so that he can talk to Yupin when she feels like conversation." Her peals of laughter were infectious, and Lamon joined in.

"Na, Na," called Boontom as she leaned out of the window again. "Come here and meet another one from Lopburi province."

In walked a woman who, Lamon guessed, was a few years older than herself. Her hands were clawed and gnarled, the skin of her face wrinkled.

I suppose I look like she does, thought Lamon.

"Na comes from Saraburi province," said Boontom, continuing the introductions, "and Lamon is from Tha Wung district of Lopburi province," she added as Na sat down on Yupin's bed.

"Na is going to marry Mr Poot, who comes from Singburi province," whispered Boontom confidentially. "He's the clerk for the leprosy outpatients department."

Lamon stared unbelievingly at Na. "You're going to be married?" she said in a questioning tone of voice, thinking she must have misheard.

"Yes, I am," answered Na cockily. They all laughed, knowing exactly what was going on in Lamon's mind.

"We leprosy patients can get married, you see," continued Na. "You look as bad as I am, but who knows, you may find someone here who will fall in love with you."

"We shall have to introduce her to those three fellows from Saraburi," said Yupin, now taking greater interest in the conversation.

"Oh yes, Wisut, Boonlerd and Tawat, you mean," said Boontom. A burst of girlish laughter filled the room.

Lamon was still standing where the nurse had left her. She turned to look at the bed which the nurse had indicated was hers, and then walked towards the bed-side locker. "Is this my cupboard?" she asked, glancing round the room and noting that the others each had a similar one.

"Yes, it's yours," they chorused. "We all have to have our private cupboard to keep our things in."

"I don't need much space," commented the new-comer. "I have very few possessions."

"Oh, but you'll soon accumulate all sorts of things," said Na. "We all do."

"Little sister, are you all right?" a male voice interrupted their conversation. Samart stood at the door.

"Yes, I'm fine," answered Lamon. "This is my older brother," she said to her new friends as he came into the ward.

Samart felt pleased that his sister was already making friends. "I have to go now," he told her. "I'm sure you'll be all right. I'll come to visit you again next week. Don't worry about anything, these people will help you and explain about anything you don't understand."

"Yes, we will," they all assured him.

Beds with mattresses, clean white sheets, decent plates and cutlery. A real toilet, a bathroom where water came from a tap. Decent food three times a day. Freedom to come and go as she liked without any fear of derogatory remarks being flung at her. Lamon was almost in a trance for days on end after her arrival at Manorom Christian Hospital.

And this light that came on every night - an electric light they called it! "What is 'electric'?" Lamon asked. "Where does it come from?" At twenty years old she had never heard of electricity.

And the people - the other patients on the leprosy wing. From the moment she arrived they came to chat with her as though they had always known her. She felt accepted and loved by them. She was one of them and they made her feel secure. Yes, she was one of them because they all had leprosy. They were mostly deformed and had ugly skin and ulcers on their feet. They were not afraid of each other, because their common disease made them all look alike.

But it wasn't only the outward appearance that brought the kinship and sense of security. Ugliness, deformities and disease should surely have made the patients depressed, dull, dejected. But they were the happiest people Lamon had ever seen. She really couldn't see what they had to be thankful for, and yet most of them were thanking God for everything.

"What are you doing?" Lamon asked Mrs Boontom the first morning. She crossed to look more closely at the handwork her new friend was doing as she sat in bed.

"I'm embroidering a traycloth." She spread it out for Lamon to see.

"But how can you do it when your hand is so badly damaged?" asked Lamon. "It's beautiful!"

"Watch me." Boontom proceeded with the slow, tedious work. "Miss Molly will be coming round soon. I imagine she'll give you something to do. She'll help you and show you how to do it, even though both your hands are so bad."

"Who's Miss Molly?"

"She's in charge of the Rehabilitation Department. She's full of good ideas and trains us to do various kinds of handwork. She's hoping that my work will be good enough to sell before I leave hospital. Then I can do embroidery at home, send the pieces here as they are finished, and she'll send money to me as wages for my work.

"Molly's a foreigner from England," Boontom added. "But she speaks our language very well."

Lamon's mind was buzzing with questions. "How will you send the work to her when you've done it? And how will she send you the money?"

"When my husband goes to Ban Mi leprosy clinic to collect medicine for me, he'll take the finished work and give it to the nurse. The nurse comes here to Manorom quite often so she'll bring the mats with her. Molly will give her the money and she'll take it to the clinic the following month."

"Does your husband have leprosy too?" asked Lamon, changing the subject.

"No. My disease wasn't very obvious when I got married. No one seemed to know what was wrong with me. I suddenly got worse when my baby was born."

"So what happened when he found out what was wrong with you?"

"He doesn't seem worried about it. He's very good and kind to me. He works hard on our farm, we can grow just about enough rice to keep ourselves. He seems to enjoy going to the clinic to collect my medicine, he likes to chat with other patients and he certainly isn't afraid of this disease.

"You'll meet him soon, he'll be coming to visit in a few days and he'll bring our little boy with him," Boontom added.

"How old is your boy?" Lamon enquired, taking great interest in this story.

"He's two years old."

Chapter 21
Life on the leprosy wing

I t is a thrilling miracle to see people with severe
leprosy who have been rejected by the world returning to normal. The changes in personality
during the early weeks after their admission to a
Christian hospital are exciting to watch.

Lamon was no exception. Within days she found
herself carried along with the hustle and bustle of life
on the leprosy wing. The patients often congregated in
groups along the corridor to share their experiences and
problems, and Lamon soon realized that some had had
much more difficult lives than she had.

"Come and sing with us, Lamon," invited her new
roommates one day.

"Sing!" repeated Lamon. "What are you going to
sing?"

"Come and see, we have lots of good songs. You'll
soon learn them."

Curiosity got the better of her and she followed them
along the corridor. A number of people were already
sitting crosslegged on the floor at one end of the
veranda behind the men's wards.

The songs turned out to be Christian songs - of all things! And yet Lamon had to admit to herself that she enjoyed the singing, and even the words and meaning of what she sang.

The gatherings were not just religious meetings, but also times of fun and laughter. One man, Mr Riab, possibly the most deformed patient of them all, was the life and soul of every party. They laughed and laughed at his jokes, they actually teased him mercilessly about his deformities, but he just laughed with them.

His singing voice was atrocious. "He sounds like an old buffalo when he sings!" someone commented. Yet he was a most gifted verse writer. His poems, taken from the Bible, were set to Thai music to make authentic Thai Christian songs. As often as possible Mr Samyong the lab technician who had been a theatrical star, would come to the leprosy ward to accompany their singing on his *renard*, a popular Thai musical instrument.

"Good morning, Lamon," said one of the older men in the group as she took her seat among the others.

"Good morning," she replied, wondering who this could be who knew her name without being introduced.

"I'm Ploog from Lopburi," he informed her. "I saw your brother yesterday, and he told me that he'd just brought you here. I'm very pleased to meet you at long last."

"Are you the Mr Ploog who's had the new nose?" she asked, overjoyed to meet this man after all she had heard about him from Samart.

"That's right," he chuckled. "I'm here for one of my frequent return visits to try to get the infection in my nasal cavity cleared up.

"I'm delighted that you've come to hospital," Ploog

continued. "I've been praying for you for a long time, that you'd be able to get here and have more treatment for your leprosy."

After singing and prayer, a Bible reading and discussion about what they had read, followed by yet more singing, the group began to disperse. But Boontom was keen to make sure that Lamon was introduced to as many "southern" people as possible. So she quickly called Wisut before he and his friends could disappear.

"You must be Samart's sister," said Wisut. "I was talking to him yesterday."

Lamon thought Wisut must be a little older than herself. She could see that he too had lumps and bumps all over him. His face was flushed as though with fever, and occasionally he winced when he moved his arm.

"Wisut and Boonlerd are both from Saraburi," said Boontom.

"How did you find out about this hospital?" asked Lamon.

"We go to the mission leprosy clinic in Saraburi. Nurse Eileen recommended that we come here because I'm very unwell sometimes, and Boonlerd has bad ulcers on his feet. That's why he has to move around in a wheelchair all the time."

"Everyone talks about Nurse Eileen," remarked Lamon. "My nurse at Lopburi is called Eileen too."

"Same person!" they all chorused together. "She lives in Singburi with her friend. They travel around that province as well as Angthong, Lopburi and Saraburi provinces, holding a lot of leprosy clinics."

"My first contact with these missionary nurses was at Inburi when I started with this disease at first," Wisut continued. He always enjoyed telling this story.

"Inburi!" echoed Lamon. "My sister lives in Inburi. I may go to stay with her when I leave here."

"You'll be all right then, Nurse Eileen is responsible for Inburi too."

"If you live in Saraburi, why did you start treatment in Inburi?" asked Lamon with curiosity.

"My brother had leprosy for several years before me, so when I started with the same symptoms I knew what disease I had, and was very frightened. There was no leprosy clinic in Saraburi then, but one day I heard there were foreigners in Inburi who had treatment for leprosy.

"I had a hard job persuading my brother to go with me, but eventually we saved enough money and I convinced him that I had adequate travel instructions for getting to Inburi."

"How far is it from Saraburi to Inburi?" asked Boontom.

"About a hundred kilometres," Wisut told them. "It was quite a journey. We had to get a bus from Saraburi to Lopburi, change there for Singburi and finally get a boat for the last twenty kilometres. It took us most of a day and night to get there.

"When the doctor and nurses found out we had travelled all that way they were astounded. They examined us, gave us medicine and recommended that we get treatment from Lopburi in future. Lopburi at fifty kilometres away was far enough, but better than Inburi. However, not long afterwards Nurse Eileen started a clinic in Saraburi. The medicine sala is built on my parents' land not far from my home."

"Do you live near Wisut?" Lamon asked Boonlerd.

"Oh no, I live out in the country, about fifteen kilometres east of Wisut."

"The first time Boonlerd came to clinic, he came on an elephant!" Wisut chortled. "What a mess he looked! His hair was long and matted, he was almost naked, filthy dirty and very thin. He wore great heavy boots that were much too big for him."

Lamon and Boontom looked at Boonlerd and smiled. Great changes had obviously taken place since that time!

"I rode the elephant to the clinic because I didn't have any other means of transport. I didn't have any money for buses, nor clothes to wear. And anyway, I wouldn't have been allowed on the bus."

"Where did you get the elephant from?" asked Lamon.

"I worked for its owner. He employed me to live with it in the forest. I had to ensure that it wandered about where it could find food, but didn't stray into civilized parts and go on the rampage."

"How much did you get paid?" enquired Boontom.

"The owner didn't pay me any money, he just gave me food twice a day."

"And where's the elephant now?"

"Oh, I quit that job soon after I started treatment. The nurses and other people gave me clothes and cut my hair for me. Eileen and her friend Rosa went to my home to visit my family and explain about this disease. When my mother understood that I could have treatment and wasn't a danger to the community, she let me move back to our house. Now I live in a hut in my mother's backyard."

They all fell silent for a few moments.

"Where is Tawat?" Boontom asked.

"I think he's gone to have his leg X-rayed again. The doctor says he'll be able to leave hospital soon."

"Who is Tawat?" asked Lamon, anxious not to miss anything.

"His home is in Saraburi too," Wisut informed her, "but he's been working in Takhfa. He was involved in a shooting incident and his leg was shattered. It's taken months to get better."

"He's a lucky guy!" Boonlerd interjected. "He was in the general hospital when he first came to Manorom. But then the doctor found he was starting with leprosy symptoms. They moved him into this department and he was able to have treatment immediately, so now all the outward signs are gone. He still takes the tablets but he has no deformities."

"He didn't think he was lucky when he came in this ward at first," commented Wisut. "He didn't believe that he had leprosy. He was furious and wouldn't talk to us for days. He's all right now, since the marks on his skin began to fade. He and I may travel home together before long."

As the weeks went by Lamon often thought about the truths that Samart had explained to her from the Bible. She compared the lives of the people she was now living with to those she had lived with in the temple. There was no doubt in her mind now that there was an Almighty God in control of this world. She was observing that He could make a great difference in people's lives and attitudes.

It was hard to forget her lifelong background of Buddhism, and her sense of obligation to be loyal to her country's state religion and her old Buddhist friends.

However, she knew she was changing. She was beginning to admit that what the Bible taught made sense. Her problem was not that she couldn't believe in the living God and His teaching, but rather that she would like to adhere to both religions at the same time! She realized that this was not possible - the Bible taught quite clearly that the living God is the God of gods, and has forbidden those who believe in Him to worship other gods or idols.

These were hard facts for Lamon to accept. She understood that if she became a Christian it would be a very serious decision, she could not play at it. So she hesitated. She would weigh up the facts for a longer period, and continue to observe the lives of other Christians around her.

Would she one day follow this same way as her brother and her new friends? They had all been Buddhists previously. They were all Thai subjects, and she had to admit that their new faith had not made them disloyal to their king and country.

Lamon was conscious of a power outside herself urging her to respond to God's invitation to join His family. But because of her loyalty to Buddhism she couldn't make the break. One day she must decide definitely to accept or reject the living God and His Son Jesus Christ. But not yet.

Chapter 22
Snakes and ladders

"**Y**ou must go back to Saraburi and look for your father," Wisut said to Tawat in persuasive tones. "If you can't find him, or if he doesn't want you to live with him again, I'll help you to find somewhere to live. You can stay with my family for a beginning."

Wisut had been in hospital for many weeks and was now much improved. Tawat was at last ready to leave hospital - his leprosy under control and his injured leg well and strong. These two young men, who had formed a strong bond of friendship, were delighted to be able to travel home together.

In his snakes and ladders existence, Tawat felt leaving Manorom was like being at the top of a snake - he was about to drop back to square one. So Wisut's offer of hospitality until he could find somewhere to live was God's intervention. Tawat had been worried. He wasn't at all sure where he would live if he returned to Saraburi. The thought of being forced back into his childhood surroundings was appalling to him.

"Thanks very much," he said to Wisut with a good deal of enthusiasm. "How much is the bus fare to

Saraburi?" he asked nonchalantly. He knew his finances were not good, but he didn't want Wisut to know just how broke he really was.

"Less than thirty baht," Wisut told him after some rapid mental arithmetic.

Tawat swallowed hard. "And how long does it take to get there these days?"

"The same as always. We still have to change buses in Chainat, Takhli and Lopburi, and the roads are no better. I suppose it will take most of the day."

Just as Tawat had expected. So he needed money for food and drinks as well as bus fares. His greatest hope was that Mr Dee would keep his word and return to pay the last hospital bill. He dared to believe that, as a final gesture, his ex-employer might also offer him a small gift for immediate expenses after leaving hospital.

To his relief, Mr Dee appeared two days before Tawat was due to depart from Manorom. He was able to leave with a clean conscience - he was not in debt, and the one hundred baht from Mr Dee felt like a mint of money in his pocket.

Tawat was welcomed by Wisut's family and assured that he could stay as long as he wished. But he knew that he would not continue to be welcome if he couldn't contribute anything to the budget.

"Come with me to the foreigners' house," Wisut invited Tawat one day, soon after they arrived home.

Tawat complied, though without much enthusiasm as he felt shy about meeting two foreign women. Wisut had no qualms about going. He knew the missionaries well as they had helped him when he had been very ill before going to hospital.

"Anyone at home?" Wisut called as they approached the house.

"Yes, come in," a female voice replied.

Wisut introduced his friend to the missionaries. "This is Miss May and Miss Rosa," he told Tawat with great formality, followed by a rather embarrassed giggle. Wisut didn't find it easy to take the initiative, even in the simplest matters.

But they were soon at their ease as May brought drinks and biscuits for them to nibble.

"They make these biscuits themselves," Wisut informed Tawat as he helped himself to a third one. "They are good, aren't they?"

"Yes, delicious!" agreed Tawat, himself taking another one.

"May comes from Ireland which is near to England," Wisut said, feeling quite important as he showed off his geographical knowledge. "And Rosa is from Switzerland.

"Tawat has the same disease as me," he informed the ladies. "But he's very fortunate that he was already in hospital when the doctor found early symptoms on his skin. He's been taking the medicine for several weeks and now the marks have gone.

"Isn't that right, Tawat?" he added, turning to his friend.

"Yes," Tawat had to answer, but he felt dismayed and provoked that Wisut chose to draw attention to this fact. *I hope he isn't going to tell everyone I've had this disease,* Tawat thought as a sense of annoyance crept up inside him.

During the following half hour or so there was animated conversation between Wisut and the missionaries as he talked about his experiences at Manorom. May and Rosa were delighted to find that he had obviously made progress in his Christian life. He told them about new truths he had learned from the Bible, and was obviously overjoyed with his new Christian friends and the fellowship they had had together. May and Rosa hadn't been absolutely certain that Wisut was a real Christian before he went to hospital. Now there seemed no doubt.

"I'm glad to be back in time for our Saraburi clinic next week," Wisut commented. "I'm looking forward to seeing the other patients again."

"We've had good clinics while you've been away," Rosa told him. "Numbers are still increasing. Eileen was very busy last month, and she's hoping that another nurse will be able to come along every month to share the workload.

Throughout this conversation, Tawat sat in silence. His emotions were alternating between pleasure as he listened to what was being said, and dismay as he switched off for long moments because his thoughts kept going back to Wisut's statement: "Tawat has the same disease as me." *I'm still not convinced that I ever did have this disease*, argued Tawat with himself. *But even if I did, I'm better now. There's no need for anyone else to know that I've ever been infected.*

"Shall we see you both on Sunday?" May asked the young men as they got up to leave.

"Oh yes!" exclaimed Wisut with great enthusiasm. "We know lots of the Christian songs now. I'm looking forward to the meeting. Thank you again for the biscuits," he added, "they are delicious."

"Thank you," echoed Tawat, knowing he must show courtesy in spite of his uneasy mood.

Wisut was quite unaware that he had upset his friend. He chatted nonstop as they walked away, and his obvious sense of exhilaration helped thaw out Tawat's feelings.

"I know someone who owns pedicabs, he hires them

out for 15 baht a day," Wisut announced, suddenly changing the topic of conversation. "Shall we go to see him? He may be able to let us have one for a day sometimes. We could share the cost between us for a beginning, until we get some practice at riding it.

"It's hard work," he continued. "But if we find we can cope with it physically and make a little profit, then eventually we could ask to hire one each regularly."

"What a good idea!" exclaimed Tawat, brightening up considerably.

"Have you ever ridden one?" enquired Wisut, noticing his friend's enthusiasm. "It really is hard work, you know. It will make you ache all over for the first few days, and you may get saddle sore."

"No, I've never ridden one, but we need to earn some money somehow. We'll just have to bear the discomfort until we get used to it. The physiotherapist said I need to keep my leg well exercised, so pedalling a trike should do it good," Tawat said philosophically. "It may be more difficult for you than me, you're very thin and not yet better from the disease."

"Yes," agreed Wisut. "We'll just have to try it out."

So the same evening they went to make enquiries. The pedicab owner told them that his trikes were all booked on a regular daily basis. "However, the men do take a day off sometimes," he said. "If you want to wait around for an hour or so they'll all be in, and I shall know if any are available for tomorrow."

They waited, but no one cancelled.

"All you can do," the owner told them, "is to come back each evening about this time, and whenever I have a free one you can use it. Or you can take one now if you like," he added as an afterthought. "You can have it for ten baht, but bring it back by midnight. You probably won't get many passengers in an evening, but you should find enough to make a few baht profit."

The two men quickly decided it was worth a try.

"And even if we don't make a profit this first time," Tawat commented, "it will be good to have some practice and get used to riding it."

"Yes, and it's much cooler at night, of course," enthused Wisut, who knew how exhausting the job could be in the blazing sun.

They paid the ten baht, chose one of the better-looking cabs and were off. Tawat requested to do the pedalling and Wisut was pleased to sit back and take his ease in the cab.

First they went to Wisut's home, ate their evening meal and then changed into shorts and old shirts. They were back on the main street in no time. During the remaining five hours before midnight they found a number of passengers. Their takings were sufficient to pay the hire cost and make a tiny profit.

This was the beginning of a regular job, mostly evenings but sometimes during the day as well. As they could charge their passengers only one baht per kilo-metre they had to cycle a long way to make a living.

Eventually Tawat went home, and found nothing much had changed. His father was quite indifferent to Tawat's sudden reappearance, seeming to take it for granted that if his son was back in Saraburi he would live at home. So Tawat was free to come and go as he pleased, sleeping and eating at home as it suited him. His father never pressed him to give details of his experiences. But the adult Tawat found it easier to have some kind of relationship with his father, and by degrees was able to tell him something about those intervening years.

Tawat did not exactly enjoy living at home, but it

was a relief to be accepted by his father and have freedom to go there when he wanted to. He could now visit Wisut frequently without being totally dependent on Wisut's family.

As time went by, Tawat found he had an unexpected problem. He kept forgetting to take his leprosy control medicine. While still in hospital he had decided it would be better to accept the tablets, even though he wasn't convinced he had leprosy. He certainly didn't want those lesions to reappear. After all, he had lived on the leprosy wing for a considerable time, and must surely have picked up some germs from other patients!

A month after his discharge from hospital, he was due to get a new supply of tablets from the clinic. But he found that he still had at least half his pills left! Because he had no deformities, he was not dogged by fear, and felt no need for treatment.

He didn't dare tell the nurse he had tablets left over, so he just took what she gave him each clinic. Gradually he accumulated masses of tablets. He tried hard to remember and for a few days after each clinic he did better, but always lapsed again.

In his heart, Tawat continued to have faith in God. However, he quickly realized that it was one thing to be a Christian while staying in Manorom hospital, but very different in hostile Saraburi market. The men he now rubbed shoulders with were degraded and evil, with dirty minds, bent on making money by gambling or by any dishonest means they could find. Life was going downhill again, and he found his old depression coming back more frequently.

Again he began to withdraw. He was grateful for a friend like Wisut, and also that he could go and visit the missionaries if he chose to. But he eventually found that his association with Wisut and the missionaries only made for more problems.

Wisut had severe leprosy, so it was obvious what his disease was. Tawat honestly wanted to be a friend to Wisut; he liked him very much and they enjoyed each other's company. However, sometimes Tawat had to answer straight questions about why he was friendly with Wisut. He never admitted that he himself was suspected of having leprosy, so he would make excuses and even tell lies about where they had met and why they were friends.

He had ventured to tell some of his pedicab-driver mates that he was a Christian. Some days his faith was strong and he was very courageous in talking about Jesus. At other times he just couldn't open his mouth even though there were opportunities to explain about God. He didn't so much mind being ridiculed for Jesus' sake, but when people called him "a child of the foreigners" because they saw him going to the missionaries' house, that was too hard for him to take. So he didn't go there very often. It must have looked as though Tawat were backsliding, but in his heart of hearts he was continually thankful to the Lord. He never lost his assurance that he was a child of God.

Tawat always looked forward to clinic days. The *sala* near Wisut's house was in a quiet area well out of town. He could go there without being seen by other pedicab drivers. To go to the clinic, meet the nurses and May and Rosa, sing the songs, see Wisut and Bunlerd, help in witnessing to other patients, was the highlight of each month. *Why can't life always be like this?* he wondered. But it couldn't - he had to earn a living.

Chapter 23
Tawat forgets, and grows

"**W**ould you like to go to the Believer's Conference?" asked Rosa one clinic day.

"The Believer's Conference?" chorused Wisut, Tawat and Bunlerd. "What is it? We've never heard of it."

"It's a four-day long weekend when Christians from all over Central Thailand, mostly people with leprosy, come together in Uthai. Uthai church provides accommodation and many friends help to prepare food. A special speaker comes to take meetings and you'll learn new things from the Bible and have wonderful fellowship. Everyone who goes always enjoys it."

Their appetites were whetted, and they looked at each other with eyes full of excitment. They knew they would meet many of the friends they had made in hospital.

"Of course we'd like to go," said Tawat with his characteristic little giggle, sounding more enthusiastic than Rosa had heard him for some time.

"But we don't have any money," said Bunlerd in a

tone of disappointment. "The bus fare would be expensive. How can we go? And look at my clothes," he
continued, "only rags, but they are all I possess."

These problems were soon solved. Rosa had second-
hand clothes for giving away, so she could fix Bunlerd
up with a better-looking outfit. And money from a
special charity fund could pay the bus fares for all three
of them.

The conference was a tremendous boost to young
Christians. Hearing the testimonies and problems of
others, sharing their own difficulties, listening to the
special Thai preachers exhorting them to be courageous Christians in their everyday lives - it was all just
what they needed. Their lives were different when they
came home after that special weekend.

"I would like you to pray for a young woman who
works near my house," May told the men one clinic
day. "She's young and very pretty, but I'm afraid she
may have leprosy. The nurse is going to see her this
afternoon after the clinic."

Yes, they agreed to pray for this young woman. In
fact, they were very interested in young women gener-
ally! And if she turned out to be a new leprosy patient
- she might be a suitable match for one of them!

That afternoon Nurse Eileen went with May to her
landlady's home. Ganya had been taken into this bet-
ter-off home from a rather poor family. She was fed and
clothed, but she had to work very hard for long hours.
There was no spending money and she was not free to
go anywhere.

"Your aunt has had leprosy for a long time, hasn't
she?" Eileen commented to Ganya.

"Yes, she's a severe case."

"Have you often been in your aunt's house?"

"Oh yes, she's my mother's elder sister, and she lives just next door, so I go in and out all the time when I'm at home."

"This mark on your thigh is only a very early stage of leprosy," Eileen explained, "but I would like you to take the treatment. It will kill the germs and prevent the disease spreading all over your body."

The young woman readily agreed.

As Ganya wasn't free to go to the clinic, the question was how she would get the medicine. The nurse might not have time to take it for her every month. When Tawat and Wisut and a couple of other young men heard about this need, they were extremely anxious to help, vying with one another as to who would take the medicine month by month. They were all keen to get to know this pretty young lady!

Tawat was uneasy. When he rode a pedicab, he found that his left hand was weak and couldn't grip the handlebar properly. As time went on he couldn't feel the handle with a normal grip; he had to grasp it tightly so as to be sure he had control of the trike. In his heart he knew what was happening, but for a while he tried not to believe it. *I must have injured it,* he told himself. *There must be a lot of pressure on my arms as I ride around on this trike so much.*

But as weeks passed he could not deceive himself any longer. His third and fourth fingers were beginning to curl over. He had no control over them - they wouldn't straighten out however much he willed them to.

Darkness and depression began to close in. *Why, oh why, didn't I remember to take the leprosy control tablets?* he asked himself miserably. He had heard other patients being scolded because they forgot to take their medicine; the nurse often warned people of the consequences of irregular treatment. Now here was the proof that the doctor had been right. Tawat really did have leprosy.

I'm a fool! Why didn't I trust the doctor? Why didn't I accept what he said? Then maybe I would have been able to remember to take my tablets. But it was too late to ask why. He was in anguish, dread and fear keeping him in bondage day and night. Visions of some of the older patients he had met at Manorom swept across his imagination - men like Mr You from Uthai province who didn't have any fingers.

"Please God, give me another chance," he prayed. "Please help me to remember to take the tablets regularly from now on, and please allow them to work in my body so that I shan't get any worse than this." Perhaps it was a selfish prayer, but he was desperate. In fact, as he prayed about his physical condition, God was able to speak to him and remind him that so far he wasn't a very faithful Christian.

Tawat was tempted to show the nurse his hands without admitting that he had often neglected his treatment. But finally fear drove him to be honest.

"Please look at my hand," he said to her at the next clinic. Eileen's heart sank as she examined his fingers. He winced as she exerted gentle pressure on the thick, ropey ulner nerve which she could easily locate at his elbow.

She looked at him with great sympathy in her eyes, and wasn't sure what to say for a few moments. Then she started to try and encourage him as she realized how anxious he must be feeling.

"Er, er," Tawat began hesitantly. "I have something

to tell you ... Sometimes I forget to take my tablets, so I haven't really been having regular treatment."

Frustration and disappointment came over Eileen as Tawat blurted out these words. She did have to speak severely to him and scold him, but in her heart she was hurting with him. She knew that he had never accepted the fact that he had leprosy, and this was why he had been careless about his treatment.

As she exhorted him to be more diligent in future, she took the opportunity to address all the patients waiting in the clinic, explaining to them yet again the importance of regular treatment.

Finally Eileen was able to give Tawat assurance that he could still hope for recovery. "If you will take the treatment as instructed from now on," she told him, "there's no reason why it should spread any further. You won't become like some people you've seen at the hospital. They have these severe deformities because they started with leprosy long before treatment was available. So try not to worry, Tawat, just make sure you remember to take the tablets."

Wisut's leprosy was gradually coming under control. He was feeling much better and stronger, and also looking much better. The typical "lion face" appearance of leprosy that had threatened him earlier had gone. He was relieved to find that people didn't stare at him so much nowadays, so he concluded he must appear more normal.

He had another reason to think that he must be looking better these days. What had started off as good fun between Wisut and his friends was now becoming a serious friendship between Wisut and Ganya. He'd managed to find out what times of the day she had least work to do, and sometimes she was able to let him know when the landlady was going to be out. On such occasions he was a frequent visitor, and Ganya seemed very responsive.

Eventually he confided to the missionaries that he and Ganya were seriously considering marriage, whenever he could get enough money. Even though Ganya was a lovely girl in character as well as in appearance, May and Rosa were disappointed that Wisut was not going to marry a Christian. But there was nothing they could do about it. The parents had been told and everyone approved of the match, they were socially suitable for each other and arrangements were going ahead.

Ganya was not deliberately against being a Christian, but she had neither time nor opportunity to learn about Jesus. She was still working very hard for long hours, and was not free to attend meetings regularly. Wisut assured the missionaries that he was already explaining to Ganya what it meant to be a Christian. He was convinced that once they were married he would be able to teach her and eventually she would become a Christian. In the meantime she had no objections to him being a Christian.

The missionaries were not at all convinced. But they had to pray for the couple and trust God as the wedding plans went ahead.

At the Believer's Conference Tawat had heard about a new project being set up at Manorom. He had had no hope then of being eligible to take part in it. But now he was beginning to wonder. His hand was only slightly crippled, but he might just be accepted.

"Do you know anything about the new training

programme at Manorom Leprosy Rehabilitation
Centre?" Tawat ventured to ask Eileen one day at the
clinic.

"Yes," she replied, "it seems to be functioning very
well. Some men have already moved in and the first
course has started."

"Do you think I should qualify for one of the
courses?" Tawat asked, "or does one have to be much
more deformed than I am?"

The nurse hesitated. She knew that the idea of the
rehab centre was to cater for those who could not work
normally because of their leprosy.

"I understand that the programme is mainly for
people who are worse than you," Eileen began. "Rice
farming is a very unsuitable occupation for men with
numb feet - and yet so many of the patients are farmers.
Their feet and hands have got much worse because of
their work, and yet we can't really forbid them to work
on their farms if they don't know how to do anything
else. No one would employ them because of their
obvious leprosy.

"I know that you don't have any regular work, but it
isn't because of your leprosy, is it?" she continued.
"You're a strong young man and if work was available
you would easily learn how to do it. Your slight deformity in this one hand is hardly noticeable, and wouldn't
be a hindrance to you in finding work."

Eileen was concerned for Tawat, however, and felt
that it would be good if he could learn some kind of
trade.

"I'll make enquiries for you," she told him. "Even
though you're not badly crippled your hand is abnormal, and it would be good for you to learn how to handle
tools with that impaired sense of feeling in your hand."

Tawat's hopes soared, and a big beam spread across his face.

"I can't make any promises," she continued quickly, "but I will speak to Molly about you. If the course isn't full with men who are worse off than you, then you may be accepted."

For the next month Tawat felt as though he were walking a tight rope. He dare not let his hopes soar too high, and yet it could just be that he was about to step onto the first rung of another ladder.

The days until the next Saraburi clinic seemed endless to Tawat. But at last the day came, and with it good news. The nurse brought an application form for him to send in to the Rehabilitation Centre, and a message to say he would probably be accepted in the next group of trainees.

From then on things moved rapidly. Tawat visited his friends at Manorom, had an interview with the staff at the Rehabilitation Centre, and was accepted to start training in the shoemaking department for the next session. He looked around the rehab building, saw the workshops and met the men who would be teaching him.

The shoemaking department was always busy as many of the shoes made there were specially for leprosy patients - fortified with thick cellular rubber soles to give protection to patients who have no sensation in their feet. Because of abundance of work, Tawat was allowed to stay on after his six months' training period ended.

For Tawat this period at Manorom was a time of weighing things up and of realizing that God had a plan for his life. He felt he would like to know what this plan was.

Ever since he had trusted in Jesus Christ his life had been rather aimless. One problem was his sense of inferiority, especially when asked to read passages from the Bible. Reading wasn't one of his strong points - how he regretted all those years of playing truant from school! However, being at Manorom gave him opportunity to study the Bible thoroughly with help from more mature Christians, as well as attend regular evening Bible School sessions. So Tawat's spiritual appetite was stimulated. Even though he wasn't the brightest student in the class, the teachers didn't seem to think he was hopeless. They encouraged and helped him as much as possible.

"Why do you want to go to Bible School?" asked Mr Poot.

"To study the Bible, of course!" Tawat answered a little sharply, feeling somewhat threatened as Poot seemed to be challenging his motives.

"It will be hard work, you know. It's not a holiday, or a place to use up a bit more time because you can't get a job. You have to do regular manual work on the school farm to supplement your fees. Also you will have to keep your nose to the grindstone with the study. I suspect you won't find it easy."

"I realize that. I've thought about it a lot," Tawat answered. "I hope God will help me to be diligent and persevere. I've twice been a Buddhist monk, you know. We had to study then and I was able to stick at it." If he was in an environment where others were studying, Tawat was sure he could cope.

Before being accepted at Khon Kaen Bible School, all prospective students had to have their application form signed by leaders of their home church to guarantee that they were Christians in good standing. So Tawat was interviewed by the leaders of Manorom Leprosy Church.

"They're very strict about morals, you know," said Mr Gen, one of the senior workers in the shoe department. He knew Tawat very well and sometimes felt anxious about his way of life, although he had no evidence that Tawat was involved in anything really wrong.

"Are you afraid that I go drinking when I go into the market in the evenings?" Tawat asked with a laugh. "You've never seen me drunk, have you? And I'm never very late back.

"Don't worry about me," Tawat continued as he looked around the group of men. "God will help me to keep straight and work hard. Please pray for me that I won't let God down, nor you people of Manorom Church either as you sponsor me."

"Let's sign the form for him," said Mr Arporn finally. "I've known Tawat for a long time. I believe he's genuine and has real faith. I knew him before he was a Christian. I can trust him and trust God to care for him and keep him from temptation."

The form was signed and posted. If the school accepted Tawat as a student, he would be able to start in April, 1968.

Chapter 24
Lamon at home

"**M**y name is Margaret. I'm the new nurse, come to replace Eileen. What's your name?"[1]

"My name is Lamon. I'm pleased to meet you. How long have you been living in Thailand?"

"About five years," I replied. "I used to live in the district of Wiset in Angthong province. Now I live in Chainat town with Nurse Kay, and I'll be coming to help in Inburi clinic every month."

"That's good, I hope we shall be good friends. You must come to visit my home one day. I live with my sister just a short bus ride away from this *sala*."

"Thank you very much," I replied enthusiastically. "I'd like that!"

"Nurse Eileen used to visit my home quite often," Lamon explained. "My sister and my nieces like the missionaries to go and visit. They are learning to sing Christian songs and like to listen to Bible stories. My

---

[1] *Author's Note:* This was my first conversation with Lamon. It was also early in my experience as a full-time leprosy nurse.

sister now believes in God. She's stopped giving food to Buddhist monks and doesn't go to the temple any more. But she's a very new Christian so she needs help and encouragement."

My role at Inburi clinic that year of 1966 was to act as the chiropodist. As I scraped away hard skin on the feet of the leprosy patients and did dressings for those who had chronic ulcers, I had time to chat with the patients and listen to their stories.

"How long have you had leprosy?" I asked Lamon.

"Since I was about six years old," she replied, and went on to tell me her life history and the effect that the disease had had on her and her family. "When I was twenty I was able to go to Manorom Christian Hospital for some operations. I used to have a dropped wrist, but see - I can hold it out straight now. It's strong and useful again." Lamon demonstrated as she spoke.

"I also had some operations on my fingers, but I'm afraid the results weren't as good as the doctor hoped. Perhaps I wasn't diligent enough in doing the exercises afterwards. The physiotherapist and the doctor told me how important they were, but when I got home there didn't seem enough time.

"I have to help my sister in her market garden," Lamon continued. "We grow vegetables to help make a living."

"Have you got any new wounds or chronic ulcers on your hands then?" I asked, fearing the worst.

"I'm afraid so," admitted Lamon. "I try to be careful, but I have to do this work, otherwise I wouldn't be able to live with my sister's family. I carry water on a shoulder pole from the river twice every day. As the two heavy cans swing from each end of the pole I have to grab the ropes and my hands get chafed across the palms."

Sure enough, there were the telltale ridges of hard skin across both palms, with unpleasant-looking ulcers on the outer aspect of each hand.

I groaned inwardly, feeling helpless and frustrated. I knew without doubt that prayer was the only answer to this problem. God alone could change Lamon's circumstances. *Dear God,* I prayed in my heart, *please work things out so that this nice young woman will soon be able to change her occupation and find work more suitable for these damaged, anaesthetic hands and feet.*

"Did you enjoy staying at Manorom hospital?" I asked as I proceeded to do the dressings.

"Oh yes, it was wonderful. It was like being in heaven. Everyone was so nice. We patients almost forgot that we had leprosy!" Lamon looked as though she were wishing she could have stayed there for ever.

"I was stubborn when I went to Manorom at first," she continued. "I liked the people, appreciated the treatment and even enjoyed fellowship with the Christians. But often I felt angry that Thai people would stop being Buddhists to become Christians. I used to live in a Buddhist temple so I was a very staunch Buddhist. I was furious when my brother became a Christian just before I went to the hospital."

"What's your brother's name?" I interrupted.

"Samart," Lamon answered. "He lives in Lopburi province."

"Oh, I've met him!" I exclaimed with delight. "I was staying in Lopburi about two years ago and attended his baptismal service!"

Surprise and pleasure shone from Lamon's face.

"Eventually, when I'd been in hospital for a while, I began to feel torn apart," she continued. "Half of me felt as though I should remain loyal to Buddhism, while the other half became desperate to be a true child of God. I began to understand that I couldn't be both a Christian and a Buddhist, and gradually I was able to believe why Jesus came into the world. I accepted that there was sin in my life, and making merit wouldn't get rid of it.

"Then suddenly, one glorious day, I felt quite different. I didn't want to resist any longer, my hard heart seemed to melt, I knew that Jesus was a real person, alive today. I was able to pray to Him, He helped me and changed me and filled me with peace and joy."

Lamon explained that while she had been in hospital she had sometimes helped the nurse aides to do the dressings. They'd also taught her how to scrape away the hard skin.

"If you need my help, I could do some of the dressings here for you," she offered. "Then you would be free to get on with other things."

I was impressed to see how well Lamon could manage the instruments, even though her deformed hands looked so inadequate. It was an encouraging demonstration of how the human body can adapt to abnormality.

"I understand that the Inburi Christians have a Sunday service here at the *sala* once a month. Are you able to come along?" I enquired.

"I try to come, though I don't always make it. You see, I'm still afraid to get on the bus alone. I think my face is much improved, but I daren't let the bus boy see my hands, so I have to travel with someone who can pay the money for the fare. My sister comes into Inburi market to sell vegetables most days, so I can travel with her and no one seems to notice me. Actually I'm getting to know some of the bus people. I think they realize that I've had leprosy but they are very nice and kind to me. So I hope that one day soon I'll have the courage to travel alone."

"I'm glad you're feeling more confident about travelling alone. I'll pray that God will give you the extra courage so that you can be more independent," I assured her.

Lamon's face broke into a smile of hope and appreciation. It was important to her to know people were concerned.

"I do hope you'll be able to come on Sundays," I added. "In future I'll be attending the meetings and helping with the Bible studies."

"Oh good, good!" exclaimed Lamon excitedly. "That's what Nurse Eileen did. Then after the Sunday meetings she used to go and visit in my village. I got to know Eileen very well, and if you come to visit often you'll become our good friend too."

"This is my sister Ploy," Lamon introduced as we approached the neat little house on stilts.

"Come upstairs," Ploy invited as she led the way, holding her small baby.

I discarded my sandals and stepped into the foot bath at the bottom of the steps. Even though the water didn't look too clean, it was cool and refreshing for hot, dusty feet at midday.

"Have you brought the song book and some pictures?" asked one of Lamon's nieces eagerly as we sat in a circle on the floor.

"Wait a while," Lamon told them. "Let the nurse have a rest."

"Take this thermos flask and go buy some iced coffee," Ploy instructed her two eldest daughters.

"Please don't bother, water is fine," I tried to persuade them. Obviously the family could ill afford even such a small luxury.

Ploy ignored my protest, dusting out the flask and sending the girls off.

"How long have you been living here with your sister?" I asked Lamon.

"Almost two years."

"Did you find it difficult to adjust after living in the temple for so long and then being in hospital?"

"It was difficult," admitted Lamon. "I felt very self-conscious when I came at first. I was really afraid that Ploy's in-laws and neighbours would reject me and I tried to stay indoors as much as possible.

"But that didn't work," continued Lamon. "It began to cause problems with the family. My brother-in-law said I must get out and do some work, otherwise I couldn't stay here. In the end that was the best thing that could have happened, because it forced me to associate with others, and by degrees I've managed to earn my right to be here. Now they accept me. No one mentions leprosy and they don't seem to notice my abnormalities."

"Praise the Lord!" I said, and really meant it. "I'm sure Eileen and other friends have been praying for you."

"Praise the Lord," Lamon echoed. "I took another step forward this morning too. I actually went up to Inburi market on the bus on my own!"

"Oh, that's wonderful!" I exclaimed, feeling as excited as she looked.

"Yes!" Lamon's face lit up in triumph. "Ever since you said you'd pray for me the other week, I've been thinking and praying about it myself. Now that it's the flood season and the water is high we don't have any vegetables to sell, so my sister had no reason to go to the market today. At first I thought I would take my nieces to the meeting so they could hand over the fares to the bus boy and I could sit and hide my hands as usual. But suddenly I had a great urge to go on my own and risk the consequences. I believe it was God urging me to do it, because I felt only slightly nervous, not anxious and agitated as I used to be even when I travelled with my sister."

"And what happened?"

"I smiled at the bus boy and gave him the money. He smiled back and said nothing. He didn't seem to notice my deformed hand. Praise the Lord again!" she said, her face beaming with pleasure and a sense of achievement.

At that point the two little girls arrived with the iced coffee.

"It's delicious," I admitted. "It really is what I needed." They all laughed and agreed that sweet, iced, black coffee was the best thing for a hot, humid afternoon.

"Have you cooked some rice?" Lamon asked her sister.

"Yes, it's freshly done, it's still hot."

"Margaret, you sing with Ploy and the children and tell them a story while I make a savoury egg. Then we'll eat our lunch," Lamon instructed.

"There are some vegetables and those tiny crispy fish too," said Ploy. "Bring everything in, Lamon, Nurse Margaret must be very hungry."

This was the first of numerous visits that I made to the little hamlet just south of Inburi market. It was the beginning of a lasting and meaningful relationship with Lamon.

Lamon soon became more confident in travelling on

her own. Eventually she went on longer journeys, even as far as Chainat where she knew she was welcome to call in and visit the missionary nurses. Best of all, once she was in Chainat it wasn't much further to go on another bus to Manorom. What a delight it was to return to the hospital and visit her many close friends!

Christmas 1967 brought one such visit, as she joined in the fellowship and parties and had a wonderful time. Life for Lamon was beyond anything she had ever imagined or dared to hope for. Life had become normal.

During that Christmas season, Lamon made a momentous decision. For months she had considered the possibility of going to Bible School in East Thailand. She had discussed this idea with her brother and sister and with many friends, who had prayed with her about the possibility.

"Any one at home?" came a voice at the door of the missionaries' home in Chainat, early in the New Year of 1968.

The nurses were quick to recognize Lamon's voice. As we came out to welcome her we could see that she was excited.

"Have you had a nice Christmas?" someone asked as they all sat down on the veranda. Immediately Lamon launched into a long story about Christmas at Manorom.

"I've just called in to tell you," she said, eventually coming to the point of her visit, "that I've filled in the application form to go and study at the Leprosy Bible School in Khon Kaen. God has been answering our prayers and has provided money to pay the school fees.

"I've just posted the application. If I'm accepted I shall begin in April."

Chapter 25
The pieces come together

I t was the third Sunday in October, 1968. I walked into the leprosy *sala* at Inburi.

"Lamon! How nice to see you !" I exclaimed in surprise and delight.

"It's our term break at the Bible School," she explained. "Samart sent me some money for the bus fare, so I'm home for several weeks."

"Wonderful! I'm really looking forward to hearing all about your life at school." I sat down on a bench beside her.

About half a dozen people had gathered for this Sunday worship and fellowship time which included singing, sharing, prayer, reading the Bible and discussing it. It was very informal, but very encouraging for the Christians who lived in the scattered villages around Inburi.

It was midday before the meeting broke up. After all the regulars had said goodbye, Lamon stayed put. She had so much to tell! She shared the hard times she had experienced during this first term at Bible School as well as the amusing and pleasant things.

I suddenly became aware of hunger pangs. *No wonder*, I thought as I glanced at the time. "It's almost two o'clock," I interrupted Lamon. "Let's go and eat noodles in the market."

As we ate our lunch it soon became obvious that Lamon had other things on her mind she still wanted to share.

"There's a young man," she began, "who is very nice and friendly towards me. We get on very well together. He isn't deformed at all really, except for two fingers on his left hand, but that's so slight it's hardly noticeable. He started at the school at the same time as I did. I knew him a little before that, but not very well. He was working in the shoe department at Manorom for a while." Lamon seemed rather shy about sharing this information.

"He seems to find studying rather difficult, so I help him when I understand things that he doesn't. He also helps me quite a lot in practical ways," she continued with mounting enthusiasm. "He's well and strong so he does some gardening for me!" She chuckled with glee. It seemed obvious that she liked him a lot.

"Even though he's well and strong physically," Lamon confided, "I feel sorry for him. Some days he's depressed because he finds the lessons quite hard, and says he doesn't like having to sit at a desk and study for hours on end. He worries because people at Manorom warned him that it would be hard, and thinks they'll be annoyed if he fails the exams.

"I try to encourage him when he's depressed. Actually the head of the school seems to like him, and often sends him on business errands. I suppose he's chosen because he has no noticeable deformity."

I was almost bursting with excitement as I listened to this story. "What's his name?" I asked.

"Tawat. Do you know him?"

"I know who he is. I often chat with the men in the shoe department, but I don't know anything about him or his background."

"Someone has told me that Tawat likes me," said Lamon, a coy expression in her eyes. "We're good friends, but I'm sure he has no thought of asking me to marry him. After all, look at my hands." She held them out. "He would never marry anyone whose leprosy is as bad as mine. He's completely healed, he needn't tell anyone he ever had it. He could marry a completely non-leprosy person."

Samart stared unbelievingly at the letter he was reading. Was it possible that his little sister, once a wretched specimen of humanity, literally on the brink of oblivion, was now so much changed that someone wanted to marry her? Presumably her suitor was another leprous person, with similar deformities to hers ... He read on.

"... His name is Tawat, his home is in Saraburi, his father is a soldier. He's a Christian and a student with me at Khon Kaen Bible School. From this you will know that he is also a leprosy patient. I am pleased to tell you, however, that his leprosy was only very slight, he has minimum deformity of two fingers of his left hand. Nothing more. No one knows he ever had this disease ..."

"Incredible!" murmured Samart in dazed tones. Part of him wanted to leap for joy and shout out to the world that miracles could still happen, but for the moment he was overwhelmed by his memories and tears flowed uncontrollably. He pushed the letter over to Keng.

Keng found it even more difficult to comprehend what she was reading. At least he had always loved and cared for his sister, and never been put off by her ugliness. Lamon had been Keng's thorn in the flesh, however, for as long as she had known Samart. At first she had put up with the facts, thinking Samart would forget his sister when he was married. She had soon realized that it would never be so.

Now what could she say? She had considered Lamon less than worthless, lashing out at Samart in jealous anger because of the money he spent on his sister and the time he took to visit her. She had cursed Lamon, called her by the most degrading words she knew. Even when she was not particularly angry she could refer to Lamon as "that revolting, good-for-nothing creature."

Since the day long ago when Keng had first visited Lamon, before she married Samart, she had only seen her briefly on two occasions. She realized that the improvement in her condition and appearance since she came home from Manorom was immense. But now, the foundations of all her Buddhist upbringing were rocked. She had been taught that those with leprosy were to be despised and rejected, left to their own devices.

Lamon knew that she could never visit Samart in his home without permission. If she had ever turned up when Keng was there alone, the reaction would have been indescribable.

"I would like to introduce Tawat to you," the letter continued. "Please may we come to visit you soon? Also we would like to have your advice about wedding arrangements." Samart's tears were shortlived. Waves of excitement came over him as he imagined Lamon wearing a wedding dress, with her hair in an attractive style. This was more than he had ever dared hoped for, more than he had ever thought to pray for! But now he was thanking God with all his heart. Apart from God's grace and mercy, such a wonderful thing could never have happened.

Yes, he certainly wanted Lamon to come and visit, and to bring Tawat along too. He was just about to say so when he remembered that Keng might not be pleased to receive them. As he was trying to decide on a tactful way to approach the subject, Keng suddenly remarked, "You will write and tell them to come, won't you?"

The day dawned bright and sunny, as usual for the height of the hot season. The plans and arrangements were complete, the cooks hired, the food ordered. Samart was up early in the morning and hurrying off to Lopburi, carrying interesting-looking bags and packets.

He got out of the bus in Tha Pho district and hurried up the familiar hill. As he approached the Lopburi leprosy clinic, he saw that a few of his friends were already busy giving the place a thorough clean. Goy had turned up to help too - he was determined not to miss this very special family celebration. With all this help Samart could proceed to hang up the decorations he had made to change the appearance of the *sala*. The decorating was a huge success.

Samart and his helpers were so happy as they worked that the atmosphere was electric with excitement. People in nearby houses were coming out to stare with curiosity, and to find out what all this laughter and joyful commotion was about.

"Today is my sister's wedding day," shouted Samart to the enquirers. "She was sick and ugly and wretched. But now she's well, she's going to be married here today.

"Come and watch," he invited them, "I want all the

world to know that the living God still does miracles. My sister will look beautiful today. Come and watch a Christian wedding, come and see what wonderful fellowship Christians can have together!"

As he saw the neighbours coming closer to the *sala*, as the word "fellowship" crossed his lips, a great surge of emotion swept over him. Before anyone could turn away, his strong voice was ringing out again. Now he was telling them about the living God and about Jesus Christ, why Jesus came into this world and what it means to be a member of God's family.

Samart didn't really have time to hang around preaching sermons that day, but he was well known for this kind of reaction! He had become so thrilled with his own experience of knowing Jesus as a real person, that he couldn't keep it to himself.

What a day that was! Everything went according to plan, even beyond Samart's expectations. As he had imagined, Lamon looked lovely, her slim figure robed in a classical Thai two-piece made from Thai silk. Her hair, carefully and attractively styled, was decorated with beautiful orchids. Everything possible had been done to help hide any remaining marks of leprosy. Tawat must have been delighted with her appearance, but it was another kind of beauty that had attracted him to Lamon. Her beauty was more than skin deep. As her name implied, she was gentle, tender, pleasant and polite.

Tawat himself was smart and well groomed. It was the first time in his life that he had worn a tie!

As the marriage ceremony proceeded and they made their vows to each other, thoughts of the future must have gone through their minds. But the sense of joy and thankfulness to their Heavenly Father was uppermost. He alone had worked in their bodies, their lives and their circumstances to bring them together in marriage. They were a living witness of what the Almighty God can achieve in the lives of men and women.

At the end of the service, bride and groom were both presented with beautiful garlands of fresh tropical flowers. These adornments, made from buds of fragrant white jasmine and deep purple orchids, were now hung around their necks as relatives and friends prayed God's blessings on them.

The guests that day came from many districts in Central Thailand. Lopburi was chosen for the wedding because it was central and easily accessible, but also because it was Samart's home church.

As well as all the invited guests, there were innumerable onlookers, the people who lived near the *sala*. Their curiosity had to be satisfied! As Samart had suggested that morning, they saw a Christian wedding and heard challenges from the Word of God as Tawat and Lamon were exhorted to be faithful to each other and to the living God.

Without doubt, the guest who brought most joy to Samart, Lamon and Tawat was Keng. She was still hostile towards Christianity, leprosy and all who were concerned with either. But at least she was willing to attend this Christian wedding of her so-called "good-for-nothing" leprous sister-in-law. How these three longed and prayed that this might be the beginning of Keng's walk away from hostility and self-righteousness, until eventually she became a child of God.

"What's the baby's name?" I asked Lamon. It was the first time we had met for many months.

"His name is Pattana," Lamon said with great pride and satisfaction.

"Why did you give him that name?" I asked.

"Surely you can guess!"

I was teasing her. *Pattana* means *progress*. "Yes, I can guess, but I'd like to hear you tell me!"

So once again out poured the story of Lamon and Tawat's life. How God had stooped down and "picked up the pieces," put their lives together again, and was now leading them along step by step. The fact that the disease had been arrested and controlled in their physical bodies. Their continuing good health, their spiritual awakening and response to God. Their marriage, their acceptance into society. The opportunity to go to Bible school and the profitable time it was proving.

"And now I have a baby of my own," Lamon concluded. "It's a miracle! You know better than I do, that many women whose leprosy is as bad as mine was, are not able to conceive."

"True, true," I acknowledged as she paused to draw a breath.

"This is all progress," Lamon blurted out. "Progress made possible because God was preparing the way for us, and is in all these things with us.

"I'm so happy," she confessed. "Tawat is such a good husband to me. I still can scarcely believe that God could have favoured me in all these ways. Thank you God, thank you God!"

My own feelings defied description. My happiness for her was boundless. As she stood there holding her precious little boy I wanted to hug them both - and I did.

Epilogue

As the decade of the seventies dawned, thirty or more people throughout the province of Lopburi had become well established Christians as a result of the leprosy programme. They were getting the idea that it was good to meet together regularly for fellowship and teaching. With improving road conditions it was easier for people to travel. So they began to meet for a worship service on the last Sunday of each month at the leprosy clinic *sala*. A smaller group would meet every Sunday in someone's home.

For the first twenty years of OMF work in Central Thailand conversions were slow and the work of forming church groups laborious and discouraging. Now at last things had begun to happen. In Lopburi town, a small group was meeting each Sunday in the home of non-medical missionaries, Emerson and Grace Frey. Some were Christians, some came wanting to know more about the Living God. None had any connection with leprosy.

When these two groups originated, it was positively

- "ne'er the twain shall meet." Even though the doctor could guarantee the patients free from infection, the stigma of leprosy continued.

One familiar face at the non-leprosy group was Samart's. He attended as often as possible, though by no means every week. Whenever he did get there on the third Sunday of the month, he could have been heard to remark, "I won't be here next week. I'm going to join in fellowship with Christians at the *sala*."

The first time he made such a statement he was bombarded with questions. "Which sala?" "Where is it?" "Who are the people that meet there?"

So Samart and Grace Frey were able to explain about leprosy and the modern treatment for it, and to give the good news that it was coming under control.

"I know that *sala*," said Ratana with interest. "It's near my home, and I know some of the nurses who work there." Ratana was a hairdresser who had a small business in the front room of her mother's house up the hill at Tha Pho. She had been a Christian for a few years.

Samart let it be known that he was not afraid to attend meetings with leprosy people. Grace and Emerson didn't hide the fact that they too often associated with the patients. So non-leprosy Christians started to share fellowship with this group of previously despised people. Ratana and some of her contemporaries were among the first to take this risk. Perhaps they went out of curiosity at first, but once in the *sala* they recognized and came to appreciate the warm fellowship.

By 1971 this end-of-the-month meeting in Lopburi *sala* had become well known not only throughout Lopburi province, but in neighbouring Saraburi and Angthong provinces. Leprosy and non-leprosy Christians, forming a multistrata group, enjoyed fellowship together. Their aim was not just a one-hour worship service on Sunday morning - they came for the day! In the all-age Sunday School, older and newer Christians divided into groups and received Bible teaching suitable for the stage they had reached in their Christian faith. Bible memory sessions took place, and times of singing ensured that all were familiar with popular Christian songs. And of course there was the worship and preaching service.

As the meeting grew in numbers and activities, spilling over into the afternoon, it became necessary to provide a midday meal.

Was it presumption on the part of missionaries and Christian leprosy sufferers to suppose that so-called "well" Christians would eat food with "lepers" as many still regarded them?

Miracles still happen. By degrees, scruples disappeared and all were able to share in the fellowship meal.

The increase in numbers was not only among leprosy people (or ex-leprosy sufferers as they should rightly be called). Teachers, soldiers, business people, civil servants, people from every walk of life, all began to come. Most people's first reaction on attending the *sala* meeting was shock. But they continued to come. Those who were genuinely searching for the truth were not put off by leprosy.

It was 1972. At last a viable church had emerged, with a committee of leaders. One whispered to another the need for a full-time Thai church worker.

"Have you remembered that Tawat is finishing at Bible School this year?" Grace Frey asked the leprosy church committee one day. "Would he be suitable to help with evangelism and pastoral work?"

This seed thought led to long discussion before a

decision was reached. How could this small group possibly support a church worker and his family? Humanly speaking the odds were against it. However, if the group of non-leprosy Christians would contribute to a support fund for Tawat, it might just be possible. The two groups were still only meeting once a month.

Finally the "well" group decided to support the project, and Tawat came to be a full-time helper for the church in Lopburi. His ministry was mostly with the leprosy church. But after a couple of years or so, the two groups began to move closer together. Tawat was a useful liaison person when ideas about buying land and erecting a church building began to erupt.

But that is another story ...

Life was somewhat traumatic for Lamon after they moved to Lopburi. Her deformed hands gave her away as a leprosy sufferer and made her unacceptable in the first area where they lived. But eventually, when they moved to better accommodation, she found that her new neighbours accepted her, deformities and all. This was a great boost to Lamon herself, and also one more victory for the worldwide campaign of helping leprosy sufferers to be received back into normal society.

Pattana was already eight years old when a baby sister arrived for him. He has grown to be a fine young man, thoughtful and well-mannered, and now at sixteen years old has a real personal faith in Jesus Christ.

His cousin, Samart's eldest son, is a fine young man in his twenties, who has now been teaching for several years. He became established in his Christian faith while at Lopburi Teacher Training College. Like his father, he is outgoing and forthright and has no scruples when it comes to making his faith public. He is currently teaching in a country area with no church or other Christians near by. So he started a children's meeting in the village, which in turn has aroused interest in some adults. Now he also leads a regular Bible study group.

Samart and Keng have three other children, another boy and two girls, who have some leanings towards the Christian faith as a result of being well taught by their father. They have not yet made the same firm stand as their father and elder brother - any profession of being a Christian will have to be genuine, otherwise they will not be able to cope with their mother's objections and hostility. All four of these young people love to visit their Aunt Lamon whenever they can. Keng is still not a Christian, but the difference in her can only be described as miraculous. Instead of a dark, scowling face and a determination not to welcome anyone coming on Christian business, she now greets us with a smile, gives us the normal Thai courtesy of water to drink, invites us to sit down and will sit and chat pleasantly.

But the greatest miracle in Keng's attitude in the 1980s is that she is now able to accept Lamon as a normal sister-in-law. In fact, a very close relationship has grown up between them. It is thrilling beyond words to listen to Lamon tell of how Keng will visit her home, eat the food she has prepared and stay overnight.

She even seems to look forward to Lamon's visits to her home to stay overnight and eat with the family. Her fear, dread and disgust of this disease must be completely gone - she is no longer ashamed to acknowledge to her neighbours that she has a sister-in-law who used to be an outcast because of leprosy.

The most amazing thing of all is that Keng has become Lamon's beautician! She trims her hair and gives her a shampoo and set each time Lamon goes to visit. Cutting and especially washing someone else's hair means coming into close contact with that person's body. Perhaps only those who have known Keng over this long period can really understand what all this adds up to and especially what this must mean to Lamon. THIS IS TOTAL ACCEPTANCE.

Appendix I

After the exodus of missionaries from China during the communist take over of that country in the early 1950's, the name *China Inland Mission* became meaningless. But the members of that Mission were still anxious to serve God. In 1951 the CIM directors decided to set up headquarters in Singapore and send out survey teams to surrounding countries in East Asia. The findings of these teams revealed tremendous needs with wide open doors for evangelism. Although missionary societies had been working in these countries for many years, vast areas remained where the gospel had never been preached. So, instead of making His workers redundant, God showed without doubt that they could be redeployed immediately.

Hence the CIM did not die but merely changed its name and area of work, as the Overseas Missionary Fellowship emerged.

The survey team to Thailand soon realized that almost no medical work existed outside Bangkok. The few government hospitals were very scattered, and only in the largest cities. So came the decision, in 1952, to concentrate OMF's main medical thrust in Central Thailand.

Thailand is a staunchly nationalistic society, cemented together by extreme royalist loyalties and almost fanatical adherence to Buddhist tradition. 98% of Thailand's population is Buddhist. The Buddhist philosophy of reincarnation leads people to believe that sickness, poverty and other problems are the result of sin in a previous existence. Consequently, the hard things of this life are inevitable.

This kind of belief leads to indifference towards those who may be harder hit by troubles than oneself. Hence the lack of concern by the wealthy for those who live in poverty; the almost nonexistent sympathy from the healthy towards the sick.

The directors of CIM/OMF believed that God was leading towards medical work in Thailand, which would go hand in hand with the preaching of the gospel. Any practical help given would be a demonstration of what Jesus Himself taught and did. The prayer was that through care, concern and a display of genuine sympathy, some of the indifference would be challenged.

God has answered this prayer over and over again through the years. Medical work has been the tool for breaking up hard ground and preparing to sow the seeds of the gospel. It has been effective throughout all the eight provinces of Central Thailand in which OMF continues to work.

Appendix II

Ploog's visit to Manorom Christian Hospital took place in 1962 when Dr Grace Warren, experienced in leprosy and surgery, was visiting Thailand. She decided to try and give Mr Ploog a new nose.

As leprosy progresses, it plays havoc in many parts of the body, causing destruction of tissue wherever the germs are multiplying. The nose is particularly vulnerable, being an area where the bacilli exist in great profusion. The consequent disintegration of cartilage inside the nasal cavity causes the middle part of the nose to collapse. The deformity of Mr Ploog's nose would inform everyone that he suffered from the hateful and degrading disease.

A piece of plastic, like that used for making false teeth, was moulded into the shape of a Thai nose. Then, through an incision inside the top lip, the false nose was placed in position inside the nasal cavity. Eventually the plastic would be discarded and replaced by a piece of bone from the thigh, grafted permanently into the nasal cavity.

Ploog had quite a lengthy stay in hospital as he also

had helpful repair surgery done in other parts of his body, and his nose took a long time to heal. This extended stay in MCH gave him an opportunity to learn more about the Bible.

The nose operation was a success, but complete healing took a very long time. During the early months after his return from hospital, his nose often became infected. He needed much patience and perseverence, and so did Nurse Eileen, who spent hours visiting him at home, helping him care for his nose and encouraging him.

Appendix III

Leprosy occurs in almost all tropical and warm temperature climate regions including Japan, Korea, and parts of southern Europe. Leprosy is associated with overcrowding and as living standards rise, the disease becomes less common.

The exact mode of infection remains unknown. Entry via the upper respiratory tract is the most likely route, but entry through contaminated skin remains a possibility.

Only about 7% of those in close contact with leprosy would actually succumb to the disease.

There are reckoned to be ten million leprosy sufferers in the world, six million of them in Asia. However quoted figures may be unduly low because people are still reluctant to report leprosy for fear of ostracism or a restraint on their movements.